Albert Camus

Life and
Times

Albert Camus
Adele King

HAUS PUBLISHING • LONDON

First published in Great Britain in 2010 by
Haus Publishing Ltd
70 Cadogan Place
London SW1X 9AH
www.hauspublishing.com

A CIP catalogue record for this book
is available from the British Library

ISBN 978-1-906598-40-2

Interior illustrations courtesy of Roger Viollet/Topfoto

Typeset in Sabon by MacGuru Ltd
Printed and bound by CPI Antony Rowe, Chippenham

Contents

Introduction

Maman died today. Or maybe yesterday (Aujourd'hui maman est morte. Ou peut-être hier). With one of the most famous opening lines of modern French fiction, capturing the voice of a hero without intellectual pretensions or strong emotional attachments, *L'Etranger* (1942, translated as *The Outsider* or *The Stranger*), is the best selling and the most republished French novel of the 20th-century and has been translated into more than 40 languages. Usually regarded as a classic, it is one of the few novels taught in schools and universities and found on most lists of the best modern novels. Both politicians and rock stars alike allude to it.

The author of *L'Etranger*, Albert Camus (1913–1960), was born to a poor, uneducated family in Algeria. His father died when he was one year old. He was very different from the typical French bourgeois intellectual. Raised by an illiterate, impoverished mother and tyrannized by his grandmother, he was expected to quit school at 14 and join the working class, as his brother did. Albert Camus' love for his widowed mother is a recurring theme underlying his work, as is his love for the beauty of the Mediterranean world. As a journalist he was soon involved in defending the rights of Muslims, a position which led him into conflict with the Communist Party, of which he was a member for a time. There was often tension between Camus and the Communists and their supporters because he saw political causes in terms of people's lives rather than abstract ideals.

After moving to France during the Second World War, Camus worked with the Resistance and later became one of the prominent post-war Parisian intellectuals. For many in Europe he was especially known for his courageous, ethical journalism in *Combat*. He was one of the few French intellectuals to criticize Communism during the 1950s. In *L'Homme Révolté* (1951, *The Rebel*) he contrasted revolt against injustice with tyrannical attempts to create a new society through revolutions. He was concerned with justice and the morality of action, criticizing the death penalty and the concept that the end would justify the means. This made him the centre of controversy. Because of his opposition to the prevailing political climate in France, during his lifetime Camus was often judged for political reasons and some claimed that his novels were reactionary. *The Stranger* was read as a justification of 'French Algeria', as an anti-Arab treatise. *La Peste* (1947, *The Plague*) was said to have advocated a 'Red Cross' morality and avoided hard political choices about the necessary violence of war.

He felt himself neither entirely French nor solely Algerian. During the Algerian war for independence from France after 1954, he was strongly critical of the violence on both sides. He believed that the Muslim and French communities should be able to live together; for this he was again attacked on the political Left.

At the age of 44, he died in an automobile accident, less than three years after he was awarded the Nobel Prize for literature in 1957. Since his death and the posthumous publication of his unfinished novel, *Le Premier Homme* (1995, *The First Man*), Camus' work keeps being rediscovered and applied to contemporary situations. Particularly since 1990, he is often cited in discussions of French colonialism and the problems of Algeria since its independence. He was one of those made homeless by decolonization and is now occasionally hailed by Algerians as one of them.

Camus is a curious misfit, someone whose life was made up of struggle, personal dissatisfaction and recurring tuberculosis. He was far happier as a man of the theatre than as an intellectual. He disliked the role of moral mentor thrust upon him as a journalist, but continued to publicly defend many causes. He berated himself for his inconsistencies. A Don Juan who bedded many women, he lamented his inability to remain faithful. While one of the most famous French writers of the 20th-century, he was always uncertain of his accomplishments. He did not consider himself a novelist and called his fictions *récits* (narratives), *chroniques* (chronicles) and *nouvelles* (stories) – myths rather than realistic novels. He claimed that *The First Man* would be the first "novel" he had written. While he is often said to be a writer of allegories and moral abstractions, his fiction and philosophical essays are, as we will see, autobiographical in their origins and incidents.

Albert Camus in a portrait photograph taken at his first communion in 1923.

1
1913–1933: An Algerian Youth

Once the French conquered Algeria in 1830, settlers soon arrived. These were often poor people from France and Spain seeking employment, who became more attached to Algeria than to Europe. The ancestors of Lucien Camus (1885–1914), Albert Camus' father, were early immigrants from the region around Bordeaux. The family of Catherine Hélène Sintès (1882–1960), Camus' mother, came from Minorca and settled in Algeria in about 1840. Neither family ever visited Europe: Algeria was their only home. They had little contact with the Muslim population and the rich *colons* (those who came to Algeria to exploit the native population and the riches of the country). Lucien and Catherine's first child, also named Lucien, was born in 1910. Albert was born 7 November 1913, in Mondovi (now Dréan), a small town in eastern Algeria, where his father, though barely literate, had a responsible position with a wine company, supervising a number of Arab workers who harvested the grapes. He served in the First Zouaves in 1906 in Morocco, and in 1914 was called back into service. Sent to France, he was one of the first men to be wounded in the Battle of the Marne and died 11 October 1914.

After her husband died, Catherine moved with her two sons to Algiers, where they lived with her authoritarian mother.

The First Zouaves were conscripts from French settlers in North Africa. Their traditional uniform included blue jackets and red trousers, readily visible to German machine guns. Many were killed in the first months of the war. In 1915 the uniform was changed.

Camus' grandmother, Madame Catherine Sintès, had worked on a farm, given birth to nine children, and was a dominant personality. Two of her sons lived with the Sintès-Camus family. One worked for the railway and left home a few years after Catherine arrived; the other, Etienne, who was deaf, worked as a cooper, making barrels, an activity that fascinated the young Albert Camus who needed a man to replace the father he never knew. Much later he would use Etienne as a character in "Voiceless", one of the stories in *L'Exil et le royaume* (*Exile and the Kingdom*, 1957).

Camus' mother, who was illiterate and hard of hearing, worked as a charlady. Although she received a small pension from the French government, the family was very poor. They lived in Belcourt, a working-class French area bordering on an Arab quarter, in a small three-room apartment without running water or electricity and with a toilet on the landing. They did not have a radio or any books. When the children took their grandmother to the cinema, to hide her illiteracy from them she would pretend to have forgotten her glasses so that the boys would need to read the subtitles for her. Although the family were non-practicing Catholics, Albert was baptized when he was a baby. His grandmother arranged for him to take his first communion early on in his childhood to 'get it over with' before starting his secondary studies.

Camus' early essays, *L'Envers et l'Endroit* (*The Wrong Side and the Right Side*, 1937), are autobiographical and evoke the atmosphere of home, often with more emotion than he would show in his later work. Years later he called his childhood *violent*.[1] His grandmother often whipped him. He described her as a hard, rigid woman: *Above her bed you could see a portrait taken of her five years before, upright in a black dress that was held together at the neck by a medallion, not a wrinkle on her face. With enormous clear, cold eyes, she had a regal posture she relinquished only with increasing age… . It was because of these clear eyes that her grandson remembered something which still made him blush. The old woman would wait until there were visitors and would ask then, looking at him severely, 'Whom do you like best? Your mother or your grandmother?' The game was even better when the daughter was present. For the child would always reply: 'My grandmother', with, in his heart, a great surge of love for his ever silent mother.* Camus writes indirectly, in the third person (the child, not I), a result of his reticence to talk about his private life. Much of his writing distances the autobiographical using form and style. About his grandmother's death in 1931, he says: *On her last day, her children around her … She died an hour later. As for her grandson, he now realized that he had not understood a thing that was happening. He could not free himself of the idea that he had just witnessed the last and most monstrous of this woman's performances. And if he asked himself whether he felt any sorrow, he could find none at all.*[2] The lack of grief is one source for the famous opening of his first novel, *The Stranger* (1942), where the narrator, Meursault, shows no emotion on learning of his mother's death.

Throughout his life Camus spoke of a strange love between his mother and himself. He always describes her as silent and dominated by her mother: *She was frail, had difficulty*

7

in thinking... . As the night thickened around her, her mute-ness would seem irredeemably desolate. If the child came in, he would see her thin shape and bony shoulders, and stop, afraid... . He is scarcely aware of his own existence, but this animal silence makes him want to cry with pain. He feels sorry for his mother; is this the same as loving her?[3] In the first of his notebooks (which he began writing in 1935), he speaks of his mother and his early poverty: *What I mean is this: that one can, with no romanticism, feel nostalgic for lost poverty. A certain number of years lived without money are enough to create a whole sensibility. In this particular case, the strange feeling which the son has for his mother constitutes* his whole sensibility.[4]

Catherine Camus never understood her son's career as a writer and intellectual. Jean Daniel recounts an incident on Bastille Day, 14 July 1951, when Camus, his mother, Daniel and friends were celebrating. Camus told his mother that he had been invited to the President's residence (*L'Elysée*). She replied, 'Don't go, son. It's not for people like us.'[5] Daniel thought that Camus wanted his friends to hear this reply.

Jean Daniel (1920–) was born in Algeria to a Berber Jewish family. As a youth he rejected Communism and fought in the Resistance against the Germans at the time of the Allied invasion of North Africa in 1942. A journalist in France after the war, he became a good friend of Camus. In the literary magazine, *Caliban,* that he founded in 1947, Camus published several important articles and helped find financial assistance. During the Algerian crisis, Daniel thought it was necessary to negotiate with the National Liberation Front, in contrast to Camus. Daniel has been the director of *Le Nouvel Observateur*, a prominent French weekly news magazine, since its founding in 1964. He often cites Camus in his editorials. In 1999 he made a film about Camus's life, *Albert Camus: une tragédie du bonheur* (Albert Camus: a tragedy of happiness).

Camus' early life is described in his unfinished *Le Premier Homme* (*The First Man*), published posthumously in 1995. It is the story of Jacques Cormery, a character very much like himself. (Cormery was the maiden name of Camus' paternal grandmother.) Jacques describes games with friends; how as they were too poor to buy a ball they made their own with rags. They played in the cellars, where they constructed tents from old sacks, *in their own space at last when none of them had ever had a room or even a bed he could call his own.* Until Jacques was an adolescent and stood up for himself, his grandmother beat him for any small fault, and his mother never interfered. When Jacques once pretended to have lost a coin in the toilet, his grandmother put her hand down the hole, into the excrement, to try to find it. The one time Catherine tried to improve her appearance, getting her hair cut, her mother said she looked like a whore. His uncle Etienne fought off a possible suitor for his sister. This upset the boy, but he decided that the poverty and infirmities of his family *made it impossible to pass judgment on those who were its victims.* Throughout *The First Man* the narrator speaks of his great love for his mother, whom he often describes as beautiful, although she was *isolated by her semi-deafness, her difficulty in expressing herself.*[6]. It is a strange relationship, as they have almost nothing to say to each other. His descriptions of his mother's beauty are difficult to comprehend, but the relationship of mother to son was emotional, never a matter of understanding. Interestingly, Jacques, like Albert Camus, almost never mentions his brother.

He knew nothing about his father's origins, mistakenly believing the Camus family came from Alsace.[7] His mother told him little about his father. He only remembered her story about how his father, after having gone to see a public execution, came home disgusted and vomited. It is a story attributed to Meursault's father in *The Stranger* and to Jacques'

9

father in *The First Man*. At the age of 40 Jacques goes to France and visits his father's grave. He knows little about the man, who died at age 29, younger than the son now at the grave side: *In a family where they spoke little, where no one read or wrote, with an unhappy and listless mother, who would have informed him about this young and pitiable father? No one had known him but his mother and she had forgotten him.* He leaves the cemetery, feeling he has again *abandoned his father.*[8] Camus himself visited his father's grave in Saint-Brieuc in 1947, and noted later that he had already lived longer than his father had. (He was then 34; his father died when he was 29.)

Camus' family had no ambitions for him. He attended a local elementary school in Algiers, from 1918 to 1924, where he had access to books for the first time. Someone with his background would normally have ended his education with elementary school, but he was lucky in having two teachers who encouraged him to continue his studies. Schoolmates found him somewhat aloof, and already concerned with looking elegant. This was perhaps a way of hiding the extreme poverty of his family from himself and others. In Camus' CM2 class (second-year middle school, at the age of ten) he gained the attention of Louis Germain, a schoolteacher who would have a major influence on his life. Germain instilled a sense of discipline and moral, but not religious, values in his pupils. Schools in Algeria taught the history and geography of France, rather than that of the colony. In Camus' CM2 class there were 30 pupils of French origin and three Arabs. In Algeria at that time there were about 750,000 people of European origin, and at least seven times as many Arabs and Berbers.

Germain gave free lessons to Camus and a few other

students to prepare them for entrance examinations to the *lycée* (secondary school). He visited Camus' grandmother to persuade her to let the boy apply for a scholarship, which she was reluctant to do. As she had worked hard all her life, the idea of someone not working was alien to her. She could not understand much about the *lycée*, but hoped it would lead to a better paying job for Albert. His brother had already gone to work at the age of 14. Louis Germain wrote to Camus years later that until he visited the Camus household in 1924, he had no idea of the extreme hardship faced by the family. Camus was awarded a partial scholarship to the *lycée*. In order to get jobs during the summer to help support the family, his grandmother insisted that he pretend he was looking for a regular position, not a summer job, which would have been almost impossible to find.

> The elementary school prepared students for a Certificate of Studies, at the age of ten. This was the last year of compulsory education for those of French origin. Only a few students continued to the secondary system, the *lycée*, to work towards a *baccalauréat* (roughly the equivalent of A levels). The *baccalauréat* was earned in all of France and its colonies by only 2.5 per cent of the population in the 1930s.

In 1924 when Camus began at the Lycée Bugeaud, the curriculum for the French *baccalauréat* included Latin, English, maths, sciences, and history. The Lycée Bugeaud had excellent teachers and was reputed to be harder than many in metropolitan France. Camus writes in *The First Man* of often being detained for having misbehaved. At the *lycée* he met another teacher who became important to his life, Jean Grenier.

Grenier gave Camus a copy of *La Douleur* ('Sorrow', 1931), a novel by his friend André de Richaud (1907-1968), which Camus read with enthusiasm. The story has elements of suspense that would appeal to a young reader and contains many descriptions of the natural world. It tells of the strong love between a woman of the upper-middle class, widowed during the war, and her son, a relationship that could be considered incestuous. When she falls in love with a German prisoner, her son can only see the affair as treason; it leads to the community treating her as an outcast and indirectly to her death. While Camus' description of the novel, in an interview in 1951, is hard to reconcile directly with Richaud's plot – it *talked about things I knew: he depicted poor areas* – Camus *saw, while reading the book, that I too might perhaps have something personal to express.* Richaud's novel *loosened a tangle of obscure bonds within me.* The story of a boy and his widowed mother, towards whom he has ambiguous feelings, gave him one model for writing. He was perhaps also attracted towards the novel for its portrait of someone made into a social outcast. By the time he was 17 Camus was certain he wanted to be a writer.[11]

Jean Grenier (1898–1971) was a mystic, interested in Indian religions, a seeker of serenity. He appreciated Camus's abilities and encouraged him to write. Camus later said of Grenier's *Les Iles* ('The Islands', published in 1933): *I already wanted to write at the time I discovered* Les Iles. *But I really decided to do so only after reading this book.*[9] The older friend mentioned in *The First Man* is based closely on Jean Grenier. Of him the narrator says, *you opened for me the door to everything I love in the world.*[10]

At the *lycée* Camus was part of a different social and intellectual world from that at home; *there was no one he could talk to about his mother and his family. In his family no one he could talk to about the* lycée.[12] In a notebook entry in 1945, describing a possible *novel* about a poor childhood, Camus wrote: *I was ashamed of my poverty and of my family... . I experienced this shame only when I was sent to the lycée. Before then, everyone was like me.* He realizes, however, that

I should have needed a heart of exceptional and heroic purity not to suffer from the days when I saw on the face of a richer friend the surprise which he could not manage to hide at the sight of the house where I lived.[13] He enjoyed physical activity and played goalkeeper for the school's football team and for the Racing Universitaire Algérois junior team (Algiers University Racing Team). In later years he spoke of the happiest days of his life being those when he played sports or worked together with others in a team. In his essays he often celebrated the warmth of nature in the Mediterranean world. He later wrote that he only knew what misery was after he went to Paris and saw poor people living in a cold climate.

During the school year 1929–30 Camus passed the first part of the *baccalauréat* examination, but in December 1930 he was diagnosed with tuberculosis. His illness would influence the way he saw life; constant awareness of death was important to his philosophy. As a son of a soldier who had died in combat, he was treated for free in a government hospital. Camus described his stay in the hospital in an unpublished essay written a few years later. He hated the atmosphere, the smells, and the conversation of the other patients. He did not share their concerns. *They tried to see their future with hope. One of them had a fever of only 100 in the evening instead of 101. Another knew someone with third degree tuberculosis who was dead at 70. This was how they lived, fearing only their death, wanting to have the same death as everyone, a death that arrives in a far off future.*[14]

While he was recuperating, Camus moved to the apartment of an aunt and uncle. Catherine's sister Antoinette was married to a butcher, Gustave Acault. They were better off, and were of assistance to Camus as he continued his studies. He noted in his journal many years later: *Essential difference*

13

when I went to see my uncle. At home, objects didn't have a name. We said: the soup plates, the pot on the mantelpiece, etc. At his house: The Vosges glazed earthenware, the Quimper service... . etc. I awoke to the idea of choice.[15] More importantly, Gustave was a cultivated man and had many books in his house. There Camus read Proust and Gide. Through the influence of Grenier, he also read widely in European literature, as well as Indian literature in translation.

André Gide (1869–1951) and Marcel Proust (1871–1922) are the major French writers of the first half of the 20th century. Gide's *Journals,* **his work set in North Africa and his espousal of left-wing causes before 1936 were an influence on Camus's early thought. Camus adapted some of Gide's work for the theatre, and later met Gide in Paris. Proust's** *Remembrance of Things Past* **is often considered the greatest French novel of the 20th century. Camus later praised Proust's creative will and the effort that his long novel demanded of an ill person.**

By October 1931, the tuberculosis went into remission. Camus passed the second part of the *baccalauréat* examinations in June 1932, and following that began advanced studies, first in a preparatory year at the *lycée*. During that year, he met Claude de Fréminville.

In 1933 at the *lycée*, Camus won the first prize for French composition and the second prize for philosophy. Grenier commented however that Camus did not have a systematic mind for philosophy. In *Sud*, a magazine founded by a school friend, he published a few articles in 1932 (rather closely related to student essays for the *lycée*), among them one on the 19th-century French poet Paul Verlaine, and one on music. Around the same time, Camus was also part of a group that published *Ikdam*, dedicated to raising Muslim consciousness and advocating equality for the Muslim and French Algerian populations.[16] Camus' interest in democratic reforms for the Muslims continued throughout his life.

In 1933 he met Edmond Charlot (1915-2004), also a student of Jean Grenier, who later founded a bookshop, *Les Vraies Richesses*, and a small publishing house in Algiers, which was to publish several new writers, including Camus. Certain that he wanted to be a writer, Camus had begun keeping voluminous notes for his future projects. He was aware of his illness, and always felt he was racing against death. In a letter to a friend, he spoke of a 'work' that he wanted to create: *in four years, since my illness will hardly give me more than that.*[17]

Claude de Fréminville (1913?-1966) was from an eminent French family (his full name was Claude de la Poix de Fréminville). After he left Algeria for university studies in Paris he became the first member of Camus' friends to join the Communist Party, in 1934. Much later, under the name Claude Terrien he became a news editor and commentator for French radio after the Second World War. Camus remained in contact with Claude all his life.

Albert Camus photographed together with Pascal Pia in Lyons 1940.

2
1933–1940: Politics, marriage, journalism

Although he did not have much money for clothes, by the time he was 20 and studying at the University of Algiers, Camus had a reputation as a 'dandy'. As he did not have a scholarship for his university studies, he took on many odd jobs, especially tutoring. He studied for a *licence* (the equivalent of a BA), composed of a series of courses, in Ethics and Sociology, Psychology, Classical Literature (an examination that he had to retake), Philosophy and History of Philosophy. He worked as an art and music critic for a student publication. According to those who knew him then, Camus was reserved, seemed to feel superior, and refused to use the familiar *tu* form of address with other students. He gave the impression that his mother was mentally ill and lived in Oran. Presumably he did not want any of his friends to inquire about his family life.[18] Much later, in *The First Man*, Jacques Comery realizes, although in a different context, that he *knew shame and all at once the shame of having been ashamed*.[19]

After the *licence*, Camus wrote a *'Diplôme d'Études Supérieures'*, a sort of mini-doctoral thesis, in 1936, in preparation for the *agrégation*, the competitive examination for *lycée* teachers. The subject of his dissertation was Plotinus, Saint Augustine and the early Christian church. He may have chosen the two figures because they came from North Africa. Plotinus (205–270), the father of Neo-Platonism, was born in Egypt; Saint Augustine (354–430), an early Church father, was North African of Berber descent. The thesis contrasts Christian belief in the supernatural with Greek belief in man as the measure of all things. It is written in proper French academic style. Although his teachers considered him a good student, in 1969 a scholar established that Camus copied parts of several academic works, without citing his references, and even repeating errors they had made.[20] Camus had planned to get a post as a *lycée* teacher, perhaps in a French colony, but he was unable to sit for the *agrégation* because he could not pass the physical examination.

During 1934 while still a student, he met Simone Hié, who was elegant, from a bourgeois family, addicted to morphine and had a reputation for sleeping around. As his uncle Gustave disapproved of Simone, Camus lived for a time with his brother Lucien. Although he often said he did not believe in marriage and neither of the pair pledged fidelity, Camus married Simone on the 16th of June 1934. Some of Camus' friends thought he married Simone to try to save her. Her mother hoped Camus would be good for her daughter, and she helped them financially. From the beginning, the marriage was filled with strife. Simone was often in hospital and the pair had quarreled frequently. They took a two-week trip to the Balearic Islands in 1935 at her family's cost, a holiday which was the source for 'Amour de Vivre' ('Love of Life'), one of the essays in *The Wrong Side and the Right Side*. Camus was attracted to the Mediterranean and in particular the Spanish culture: *There is a certain freedom of enjoyment that defines true civilization. And the Spanish are among the few peoples in Europe who are civilized.*[21]

He was becoming a writer, regularly sketching his views and his plans in notebooks. At the age of 22 he would already compare his current self to how he was when 'young'. The entries in the notebooks are scarcely personal. Some express his philosophical ideas, or comment on the books which he was reading at the time. Others contain outlines for books he planned to write, or even entire passages, which he would later incorporate directly into a novel or an essay. At the time he had already completed a draft of 'Voix du quartier pauvre' (Voices from the poor neighbourhood, a first version of *The Wrong Side and the Right Side*). 'The tragedy of life, the need to construct a moral position, the distrust of rationalism, the mystique of the Mediterranean, rebellion and acceptance.'[22]

Although he was sceptical of Communism, he joined the Communist Party in 1935, as did several of his friends. Jean Grenier encouraged him by insisting that at his age Camus should try politics. For Camus the Party represented equality, a way of reducing the burdens of mankind. Even though he had written in a letter to a friend that Communism should be a religion or else it was of no use, he was not interested in Marxist doctrine, stating that the life of a man was more important than a volume of *Capital*.[23] He worked for the Party as general secretary of the Algiers branch of the *Maison de la Culture* (House of Culture), formed initially in Paris to bring cultural activities to the working classes and to advocate left-wing ideas. Camus and his companions planned to organize lectures, art exhibits, and theatre and film programmes, and hoped to attract at least some Arabs to the centre.

He also became involved with theatre, which would remain a life-long interest. He directed, wrote for and often acted in productions of *Théâtre du Travail* (Workers' Theatre), sponsored by the House of Culture. The first project was a dramatization of André Malraux's novel *Le Temps du Mépris* (*Day of Wrath*, 1935). Camus sent a copy of the script to Malraux, who replied with a short telegram: 'Play it.'[24] Camus transformed the eight chapters of Malraux's novel into two acts. The first performance was 25 January 1936. The play was performed in the Padovani Baths, a beach establishment in Algiers, which had a large ballroom (about 15 yards by 45 yards) and changing rooms for bathers. The actors were amateurs, many of them friends. They had to speak their lines between the noise of waves breaking on the nearby beach.[25] The first audience was perhaps 500 (though the local Communist Party paper said there were 1,500), and there were additional performances for several months.

André Malraux (1901-76), novelist, art critic and later politician, was a prominent anti-fascist in the 1930s. *Le Temps du Mépris* is the story of a Communist in Nazi Germany, who is saved by the heroic sacrifice of another. His most famous novel, *The Human Condition* (1933) won the Goncourt Prize. Malraux would later read Camus' first manuscripts and recommend them for publication. He was a strong supporter of de Gaulle after the Second World War, and became de Gaulle's minister of culture from 1959–1969.

Camus also wrote his first play for the theatre group, in collaboration with a friend Jeanne Sicard and two teachers, Alfred Poignant and Yves Bourgeois (with whom he would travel to Europe in the summer of 1936). *Révolte dans les Asturies* (1936, *Rebellion in Asturias*) is about how a rebellion of miners in Asturias in northern Spain in 1934, was brutally put down by a right-wing government. The rebellion, which had in fact been organized by the Soviet Cominterm, was followed by political assassinations, strikes, and preludes to the civil war in 1936, in which Francisco Franco (1892–1975) defeated the republican government. Camus felt attached to Spain through his maternal family, and continued to be concerned with its political problems throughout his life. He opposed Franco, and later American support for Franco. *Rebellion in Asturias* was conceived as epic theatre with the action taking place at a conference table in the middle of the auditorium, and the streets of the city of Oviedo, in Asturias, on either side of the audience. The idea was to give each member of the audience a personal point of view, so that the person in seat 156 would see things differently from the person in seat 157.[26]

Since the right-wing mayor of Algiers refused to give permission for a performance of the play, there would be no one in seat 156 or 157. Since there was no way to get around this ban, the only solution was to publish the play. Edmond Charlot, who was just starting his publishing business, had 500 copies of *Rebellion in Asturias* printed, which sold out in two weeks. Camus became a regular presence in Charlot's bookshop, which was a gathering place for their friends. He advised Charlot on his publishing projects and edited a series of works. Camus was already becoming involved as an editor. Later, for a brief period of time, when Charlot had problems, Camus and his friend Claude de Fréminville formed a publishing company, Cafre (using the first letters of both their names). Fréminville financed Cafre, with a legacy from his family. When he was able to publish again, Charlot took over the Cafre books.[27]

Only a few of the plans of the Workers' Theatre came to fruition. A successful production in November 1936 was *The Lower Depths*, by the contemporary Soviet writer Maxim Gorky (1868–1936). In 1937 the theatre performed an ancient

Greek drama, Aeschylus's *Prometheus Bound*, and *Don Juan* by the classical 18th-century Russian dramatist, Alexander Pushkin (1799–1837). Camus played the part of Don Juan and directed the play. Don Juan continued to fascinate him, becoming one of the exemplary 'absurd lives' in *Le Mythe de Sispyhe (The Myth of Sisyphus*, 1942). Because of his success with women, he had a reputation as a Don Juan and must have seen himself in the role.

In the summer of 1936 Camus and Simone travelled with Yves Bourgeois to Europe, visiting Lyons, Innsbruck, Prague, Vienna and Venice. For Camus central Europe was a place of exile, the reverse of the Mediterranean world he loved. In Prague, he stayed alone for a few days as he was physically unable to join the other two on a kayak trip. He was depressed and made notes towards an essay: *Prague - The first four days. Baroque cloister. Jewish cemetery. Baroque churches. Arrival in the restaurant. Hunger. No money. The dead man. Cucumber in vinegar. The one-armed man sitting on his accordion.*[28] In 'La Mort dans l'âme' ('Death in the Soul'), an essay in *The Wrong Side and the Right Side*, Camus expands on these notes. He could not understand the Czechs and had little money: *Now I can live only scrimpingly in this great city. My distress, still rather vague a few moments ago, fixes itself on this one point. I feel uneasy, hollow and empty.* He wandered in the city, tried to visit churches and museums, without any joy. *Here I am, stripped bare, in a town where the signs are strange, unfamiliar hieroglyphics, with no friends to talk to ... The curtain of habits, the comfortable loom of words and gestures in which the heart drowses, slowly rises, finally to reveal anxiety's pallid visage. Man is face to face with himself: I defy him to be happy.*[29]

During the trip, opening a letter for his wife, he learned

that a doctor who gave Simone drugs was her lover. By the end of September 1936, the marriage was over, although they only obtained a final divorce decree on the 27th of September 1940, when Camus was planning to marry again. Replying to a letter from her mother asking for help when Simone had been arrested for buying heroin in Paris in 1952, Camus wrote how he had felt 17 years earlier: *I realized that the situation was hopeless. That's why I cut myself off, although it cost me more than I have ever said to anyone.*[30] In the following months Camus found more happiness in his friendship with Jeanne Sicard (who came from a wealthy industrial family) and Marguerite Dobreen, a historian. He shared a house with them when he was no longer living with Simone. They were a couple, friends *with whom he did not have to use his masculine charms*[31], which he otherwise seems to have used often. This 'House Above the World', high above Algiers on a hill, and scantily furnished, features in several of Camus's essays written in 1936–37 and in *La Mort heureuse* (*A Happy Death*).

Another young woman joined them, Christiane Galindo, who had a discreet affair with Camus and also typed some of his manuscripts. She introduced him to her brother, Pierre, who worked for an export firm, was tough, said little, and had been in a fight with some Arabs on a beach. He became a good friend, and a model for Meursault in *The Stranger*. He later fought in the Resistance against the Germans.

In March 1937, Camus gave a talk at the House of Culture supporting the Blum-Violette bill, which proposed to give suffrage to a limited number of Algerian Muslims and was a first step towards assimilation. Camus' position was that France's civilizing mission should lead to a union of French and Muslims as part of France. In May the House of Culture published a 'Manifesto of the intellectuals of Algeria in favour of the Violette Proposal'.[32]

As he was far from a doctrinaire Marxist, Camus' relationship with the Communist Party was always troubled. More importantly, the French Communist Party (and the Algerian Communist Party founded in 1936, but controlled from France) took a line about the indigenous Algerian population that Camus could not accept. The Party was unwilling to go as far as Camus in supporting the Muslims; the fight against capitalism had to take precedence over the fight against colonial rule. Stalin, hoping to build an alliance with France against Germany, accepted French colonial policy. When Camus criticized the Party's position, its defense of colonial power and especially its condemnation of the Algerian People's Party (PPA) in November 1937, he was expelled.[33] It is ironic that later Marxists would criticize him as not being anti-colonialist.

No longer with the House of Culture, Camus formed a new theatre group, *Théâtre de l'Equipe* (Team Theatre). They received favourable reviews for their production of *Brothers Karamazov* by the Russian Fyodor Dostoevsky (1821–1881), whose *The Possessed* Camus would adapt years later in Paris. Another major production was a double bill of Gide's *Retour de l'enfant prodigue* (*Return of the prodigal son*) adapted by Camus for the theatre, and *Le Paquebot 'Tenacity'* (*The Steamship 'Tenacity*) by the French poet Charles Vildrac (1882–1971). The last play the Team Theatre produced, in March 1939, was *Playboy of the Western World*, by the Irish dramatist John Millington Synge (1871–1909). While opinions varied as to Camus's acting ability, those with whom he worked were aware of his qualities as a leader and director, and his skill in adapting texts for the theatre.

At the theatre in September 1937 he met Emmanuel Roblès, who, while studying Spanish at the university and beginning to write, was doing his military service. Roblès describes going to a rehearsal of *La Célestine*, a classical Spanish play, which was on his university syllabus. When he met Camus, he found him 'thin and pale, obviously in precarious health but full of ardour, energy and passion'. They became friends, sometimes swimming, sometimes going together to Chez Coco, a little bar run by a dwarf whose clientele included seamen, prostitutes and 'bizarre individuals'. Roblès witnessed an incident in autumn 1938, when a Communist militant reproached Camus for his 'cowardly desertion of the Party'.[34]

Emmanuel Roblès (1914-1995), like Camus, lost his father in the First World War. Of Spanish origin and from Oran, he published several of his first novels with Charlot; later in France he was a prize-winning novelist. He joined with Camus in seeking a truce in Algeria in 1956. Roblès remained a close friend, and helped Francine Camus after Camus's death. He later worked with Luchino Visconti, the Italian filmmaker, on an adaptation of *The Stranger* (1967).

Camus' productive years in Algeria were between 1934 and 1938. In addition to political activism and work in the theatre, Camus was writing several books. He was working on his first novel, *A Happy Death*, and *Caligula* (his first play, published much later in France), as well as completing two books of lyrical essays about his family, his friends, and his philosophical beginnings, both published by Edmond Charlot: *The Wrong Side and the Right Side* (May 1937) and *Noces* (*Nuptials*, May 1939).

In the five short essays in *The Wrong Side and the Right Side*, an experience such as pity for his illiterate, suffering mother, or despair at being unable to order a meal in Prague, disturbs the young man's normal acceptance of life. He sees death and beauty, suffering and joy, incomprehensibility and man's desire for clarity existing side by side. He concludes that *my whole kingdom is of this world*,[35] a kingdom that is a source of both joy and despair, not a kingdom of ideologies. It is a philosophical position that he will continue to develop throughout his work. In his preface to a republication of the book in 1958, Camus noted that, although he found the form of these essays *clumsy, there is more love in these awkward pages than in all those that have followed.*[36]

The lyrical essays in *Nuptials* celebrate man's relationship to the natural world. 'Noces à Tipasa' ('Nuptials at Tipasa') describes the Roman ruins in the Algerian village of Tipasa, which Camus visited frequently in 1935 and 1936. It is a hymn of praise to beauty and to his gods: the sun, the sea, the flowers that overrun the ruins: *Yet even here, I know that I shall never come close enough to the world. I must be naked and dive into the sea … and consummate with my flesh the embrace for which sun and sea, lips to lips, have so long been sighing.*[37] In 'Le Vent à Djémila' ('The Wind at Djémila'), he describes a visit to another Roman city. In Djémila nature is not a warm sun and sea; he feels a cutting wind that pierces him, detaching him from himself. From this experience he concludes that all that civilization can accomplish is to make us conscious of our fate. *You can be lying in bed one day and hear someone say: 'You are strong and I owe it to you to be honest: I can tell you that you are going to die'; you're there, with your whole life in your hands, fear in your bowels, looking the fool… . I want to keep my lucidity to the last, and gaze upon my death with all the fullness of my jealousy and horror.*[38] The two early books of lyrical essays are separated by only two years, but while in *The Wrong Side and the Right Side*, he speaks of misery and solitude, and the deceptions he encountered in politics and in his marriage, in *Nuptials* the mood changes; there is an explosion of sensations, a feeling of joy in spite of the presence of death.

It is difficult to remember, considering all Camus did (including the various jobs he took to support himself, and his many conquests of young women), that his health was fragile. In 1937 Claude de Fréminville persuaded him to take a trip to France in order to rest. They set sail for Marseilles on the 29th of July and visited Lyons, Paris, and several towns in the Alps. In a notebook entry in August, Camus writes: *On the way to Paris: this fever beating in my temples. The strange and sudden withdrawal from the world and from men. The struggle with one's body.*[39] He was later joined by his friends Jeanne and Marguerite for a trip to Pisa and Florence, where he felt at home in the 'Mediterranean' culture he loved. An essay in *Nuptials*, 'Le Désert' ('The Desert'), describes Camus' experience in Florence, which leads him to see his life as built on revolt against the tragic certainty of death, coupled with consent to the beauty of the earth: *The world is beautiful, and outside it there is no salvation.*[40]

He was then working on *A Happy Death*, which is sometimes close to a story of Camus' own life; the hero, Patrice Mersault, travels to Vienna, Genoa and Prague. He suffers from a disease of the lungs, from which he will die, a rare direct reference in Camus' work to his own fragile health. After Mersault kills an elderly cripple for his money, he spends some time in a House Above the World with several female friends (not well distinguished from one another), travels to Europe, returns to Algiers very ill, and dies happy because he finds peace *born of that patient self-abandonment he had pursued*; he then *returned in the joy of his heart to the truth of the motionless worlds.*[41]

A Happy Death was not published during his life. The

novel lacks narrative structure, the episodes are not well related to one another, the plot is often hazy and the characterization is minimal. There is no consistent point of view. Patrice Mersault tells only part of the story in the first person. The point of view of several other characters is unsuccessfully inserted. *A Happy Death* is a version of some themes of *The Stranger*, which Camus also began around about August 1937. The reader of *The Stranger* is immediately aware of the voice of the hero, now called Meursault, which gives unity to the narrative.

In October Camus was offered a teaching position at Sidi-bel-Abbès, an agricultural centre far from Algiers. As he needed the money, he felt he should accept the job. After he arrived in the town, however, he soon left. In his notebook, on the fourth of October, he wrote that he rejected the position, *doubtless because I saw security as unimportant compared to my opportunities for real life. The dull, stifling routine of such an existence made me draw back.... I was afraid, afraid of being lonely and of being permanently fixed.*[42] He needed time more than money; he noted in April 1938 that it took two years to write a book. He was never financially secure until he won the Nobel Prize, but freedom and a stimulating atmosphere in which to write was always to be more important than money. From December 1937 to October 1938 he worked for the meteorological services, and noted: *It is normal to give away a little of one's life in order not to lose it all. Six or eight hours a day so as not to die of starvation.* He worked regularly at his writing, which he called *my deepest joy.*[43]

During 1937 he began seeing Francine Faure, a young woman from Oran, an accomplished pianist and a student of mathematics, who was to become his second wife. Her father, like Camus's, had been killed in the Battle of the Marne.

She was studying in France and began a correspondence with Camus during the 1937–38 school year. Francine came from a close-knit, educated, middle-class family; among her maternal ancestors were Berber Jews, a group thought to have arrived in Algeria before the Arabs. Francine had a stricter upbringing than most of the women with whom Camus was involved at that time, who did not think in terms of permanent relationships. Francine became his fiancée and by 1940 he promised her marriage, without promising to be faithful.[44]

In Camus' notebooks by December 1938, *The Stranger* was beginning to take shape. An entry, late 1938, contains the opening lines: *Maman died today. Or yesterday maybe, I don't know. I got a telegram from the home: 'Mother deceased. Funeral tomorrow. Faithfully yours.'*[45] This is the voice of Meursault, and these lines would become one of the most famous openings in Western literature. Pierre Galindo's description of his fight on the beach in Oran became an essential element of the plot. In his notebooks, Camus also describes his visits several times a week to see his mother, after his brother Lucien was mobilized. As usual, she says little, another autobiographical element for use in *The Stranger*.

Among the entries in Camus's notebooks in 1938 are philosophical speculations and many fragmentary notations on the wide variety of books he was reading: *The true work of art is the one which says the least*; *In every life, there are a great number of small emotions and a small number of great emotions. If you make a choice: two lives and two types of literature.* He makes plans for what he will do during the summer: *June. For the summer: (1) Finish Florence and Algiers. (2) Caligula. (3) The summer impromptu. (4) Essay on the theatre. (5) Essay on the forty-hour week. (6) Re-write novel. (7) The absurd.* Some of these projects did not come to fruition, but the entry shows Camus' need to discipline himself: *the first thing is to learn to govern yourself.*[46] Camus needed a plan to organize his work.

By late summer 1938, he had another, more time-consuming and stimulating project. *Alger Républicain*, a left-wing paper, was founded as a sister to *Oran Républicain*, to compete with the right-wing papers published in Algiers. The publishers hired Pascal Pia as the editor-in-chief and Pia hired Camus. The first issue of *Alger Républicain* appeared 6 October 1938. Although he was a novice journalist, Camus became a close associate of Pia and was quickly given by-lines. He worked on the city desk, criminal trials, and political and economic news. Reporting on such cases as the Hodent affair, in which an innocent employee was tried for fraud, became a source for the descriptions of the trial of Meursault in *The Stranger*.

Pascal Pia (1903–1979), whose real name was Pierre Durand, was a writer and journalist who edited many major writers, as well as volumes of erotic literature. He was an anarchist, interested in surrealism and Dadaism. In 1938 he was working for the left-wing (and primarily Communist) *Ce Soir* in Paris. During the war in France, he helped Camus find a job and get his first books published. He was active in the Resistance movement, and became an editor of *Combat* in 1943, continuing in this role after the war. He quit the paper because of political and financial disagreements in 1947 and broke what had been a close relationship with Camus. Towards the end of his life he forbade anyone to write about him, saying he had a 'right to nothingness'.[47]

Camus also wrote a literary column and offered Emmanuel Roblès the chance to write a serial novel for the paper. In the year of its existence, *Alger Républicain* published more than 1,500 articles by Camus, among them a review of *La Nausée* (*Nausea*), Jean-Paul Sartre's first novel. While recognizing Sartre's talent, Camus finds in the novel a juxtaposition of a philosophy and images, but the *balance has been broken, where the theories do damage to the life.* Camus gave a more favorable review to Sartre's second book, *The Wall and Other Stories* in which, interestingly, he makes a comment that he will later gave to the hero of *The Stranger*: *we all more or less wish for the death of those we love.*[48] Camus would have a long, eventually troubled relationship with Sartre in Paris in the 1940s and '50s.

During May 1939 he published an article, 'Reflections on generosity', in *L'Entente* ('Harmony'), a weekly magazine with a moderate Arab line. Camus said that the Muslim population in Algeria had supported French policies, served in the French armed forces and showed solidarity with France, but France had destroyed all that by rejecting the Blum-Violette bill: *this people who offered their blood have been refused the right to express themselves.*[49] In June he wrote an important series of 11 articles, *La Misère de la Kabylie* ('Destitution in Kabylia'). Kabylia is the mountainous region of Algeria, the home of the Berbers, residents

Jean-Paul Sartre (1905–1980) wrote plays, novels and philosophical essays. He is especially known for his version of Existentialism: 'existence precedes essence'. Each person creates the meaning of his or her life; a person can only be defined by what he or she does. Sartre became a supporter of Communism, while never joining the Party, and was one of the major left-wing thinkers in France in the second half of the 20th century.

of the region before the arrival of the Arabs. He writes of the misery of the population, where most of the men have left to find jobs in France, where women are exhausted by their work, where children faint from hunger, where there are no doctors, no drains in the villages. He compares the salaries to those in France. He does not blame all the problems on colonialism; indeed he writes of how colonial rule has brought progress, and of how the population should be assimilated into the French Algerian population. He does not consider independence for Algeria. At the time, however, his articles brought to the attention of his French Algerian readers the need for changes in colonial policies. He was the first journalist to denounce French policy in Kabylia.

His articles about European politics show the confusion many on the Left felt before the outbreak of war. He wanted a socialist policy neither connected to the official line of the French Socialists (the SFIO) nor to the Communists. He was always against the Fascists and the Nazis, but uncertain about the Russians. At times he seems almost pacifist (a position influenced, perhaps, by his father's death in the First World War). After Munich he overestimated the possibility that Hitler might make peace.

After the declaration of war on 3 September 1939, Camus describes ironically the reactions of his fellow citizens: *The people who rush to be operated on by a well-known Algiers surgeon because they are afraid that he will be called up*. Commenting about his own tuberculosis and its impact on his life, a rare entry in his notebooks, he realizes that he should try to serve in the armed forces: *The dilettante's dream of being free to hover above his time is the most ridiculous form of liberty. This is why I must try to serve. And, if they don't want me, I must also accept the position of the 'despised civilian'... . If they don't want me to fight, it is because my fate is always to stay aside. And it is from this struggle to remain an ordinary man in exceptional circumstances that I have always drawn my greatest strength and my greatest usefulness.*[50]

As *Alger Républicain* was increasingly censored. Camus and Pia often printed citations to confuse the censors, who were capable of demanding that quotations from the 18th-century philosopher Voltaire be cut as subversive. Camus and Pia also tried to publish part of Jean Giraudoux's (1882–1944) *The*

Trojan War will not take place; the censors cut the extract, although Giraudoux was then a commissioner in the Office of Information of the French government.[51] A new two-page evening paper, sold by hawkers, *Le Soir Républicain*, was started 15 September, and Camus was made editor-in-chief. In October *Alger Républicain* was closed, partly for lack of paper during wartime. In January 1940 *Le Soir Républicain* was also finished. The government authorities, finding Camus too critical of their policies, made it impossible for him to find work.[52] In February Pia returned to France. With no money and no job in Algeria, Camus left for France on 14 March 1940, after Pia arranged a position for him with a popular French newspaper, *Paris Soir*.

Albert Camus and his wife Francine photographed on hearing the announcement that he had been awarded the Nobel Prize for Literature in October 1957.

3

1940–1943: The Stranger and The Myth of Sisyphus

Soon after he arrived in Paris, a disillusioned Camus wrote in his notebook about his probable life there: *being able to live alone in one room in Paris for a year teaches a man more than a hundred literary salons and forty years experience of 'Parisian life'. It is a hard, terrible and sometimes agonizing experience, and always on the verge of madness.*[53] He needed to think of Algeria when his life in Europe weighed too heavily upon him. His work was not interesting. *Paris Soir* was a large popular newspaper and Camus had a more menial job with the paper than in Algiers. He was part of the editorial team, doing page layout, working in the composing room, with no responsibilities as a writer. If the job was not demanding, Camus also had a less intensive social life. He wrote regularly to Francine, but also to Yvonne Ducailar, a French woman studying at the University of Algiers, who was one of his conquests before he left for France. In one letter to Yvonne: *For three months I have been cloistered - I've stopped everything to put in shape what I have to say for now (I haven't touched a woman during all this time and*

I think that's for the first time in my life).[54] He finished the manuscript of *The Stranger* by May 1940.

He arrived in Paris during the period of the 'phoney war', before the late May attack on France by the Germans. He made another attempt to join the French armed forces, and was again rejected because of his poor health. The German troops entered Paris on the 14th of June 1940. Armistice was declared 22 June, and a French government under Philippe Pétain (1856–1951) was soon established. France was divided into two sections, the northern part directly under German control, the southern part under Pétain's Vichy government. There was a large-scale exodus from Paris. *Paris Soir* moved south to Clermont-Ferrand and then to Lyons where Francine Faure arrived after Camus' divorce from Simone Hié was finalized on 27 September 1940. The wedding was celebrated in a simple civil ceremony on 3 December 1940. Among the guests were four typographers from *Paris Soir*, who gave the newlyweds a bunch of flowers; one of them remembered, years later, that 'Camus adored the atmosphere of the printing shop and was more often there than in the editorial rooms'.[55]

Before Francine came to France, Camus wrote to her in Oran, asking her to copy bits of the manuscript of *A Happy Death*.[56] One is the description of what the hero does on Sunday. This is a passage that Camus reworked in *The Stranger*. In *A Happy Death* Mersault eats eggs out of a pan, with no bread, because he had forgotten to buy any, and he cuts out clippings from the newspaper. (His habit is based on a real observation of a mental patient, which Camus described in his notebook in 1936. The patient gives Camus a letter which *contains advertisements cut out of newspapers and carefully arranged*.[57]) In *A Happy Death* the clippings are pasted *into a booklet already filled with jovial grandfathers sliding down bannisters.*[58] In *The Stranger*, they are pasted *in an old notebook where I put things from the papers that interest me.*[59] Camus cut the unnecessary detail in rewriting. Part of the power of *The Stranger* is its economy.

The Stranger is the story of Meursault, who clerks in an office in Algiers, and who describes his life simply, initially without being consciously aware of any thought or feeling. Meursault goes to his mother's funeral, where he does not conform to social expectations. He drinks coffee with milk, he smokes while sitting with his mother's coffin, he does not want the coffin opened, he does not cry. After the funeral he returns to Algiers, where he sees a comic movie and starts an affair with Marie, a young woman he recently met. He is an 'outsider' according to the reactions of most people. When Marie sees his black tie, *I told her Maman had died. She wanted to know how long ago, so I said, 'Yesterday.' She gave a little start but didn't say anything. I felt like telling her it wasn't my fault.*[60] In the following weeks he works as usual and sees Marie on Saturdays. He remarks on how the hand towel at work becomes too moist by the end of the day. To Meursault this seems of equal importance to his employer's offer of a job in Paris (which he turns down), or Marie's suggestion that they get married (which he says he will if she wants). He is only aware of his own sensations.

While spending a Sunday on the beach with Raymond, a procurer whom he has casually befriended, Meursault becomes involved in a fight between Raymond and some Arabs. Affected by the sun, Meursault shoots one of the Arabs. Imprisoned and awaiting his trial, he can only say he shot because of the sun. He refuses to admit guilt. When asked about his feelings for his mother, he replies: *I probably did love Maman, but that didn't mean anything. At one time or another all normal people have wished their loved ones were dead.*[61] When he is tried for murder, he is judged partially for his behaviour at his mother's funeral. To conventional society he is a monster, not fully human. After he is condemned to death, he rejects consolation from the prison chaplain, saying that his life has no transcendent value but it is all he has. He awaits his execution, having found peace and harmony with the external world: *I opened myself to the gentle indifference of the world. Finding it so much like myself – so like a brother, really – I felt that I had been happy and that I was happy again. For everything to be consummated, for me to feel less alone, I had only to wish that there be a large crowd of spectators the day of my execution and that they greet me with cries of hate.*[62]

Meursault knows that only immediate sensations are of value; he rejects society's moral codes. Camus commented in his notebooks in January 1936: *People can think only in images. If you want to be a philosopher, write novels.*[63] The novel is not, however, a philosophical treatise, but an ironic, often humorous portrayal of a man whom Camus later called *the only Christ we deserve.*[64] In his notebooks in 1937, Camus remarked on the ironic character of Meursault: *the man who refuses to justify himself. Other people prefer their idea of him. He dies, alone in his awareness of what he really is - Vanity of this consolation.*[65]

The Stranger is deliberately incongruous in structure; it is impossible to say clearly when Meursault is telling his story as he sometimes is speaking in the present, sometimes in the past. There are several bizarre characters: Salamano, an old man who lives with his dog, which he beats but mourns when it is lost; a woman who eats her dinner while marking off programmes in a newspaper. Camus will continue the introduction of such bizarre characters in his next novel, *The Plague*, where there is an old man whose hobby is to attract cats in the street under his window so he can spit on them, and another who measures time by counting peas as he transfers them from one tin into another.

The Stranger was unusual in the literary climate of the first half of the 20th century. Its hero was neither bourgeois nor aristocratic, neither an aesthete nor an intellectual. Like *Waiting for Godot* (1953), by the Irish writer Samuel Beckett (1906–1989), perhaps the other major work of Western literature to attain such a degree of influence in the post-Second World War world, it is not concerned with a hero who expresses himself with eloquence. Camus described his hero as *a poor and naked man enamored of a sun that leaves no shadows. Far from being bereft of all feeling, he is animated by a passion for the absolute and for truth.*[66]

The Stranger continues to appeal to a wide variety of readers. It has become a classic, engaging in the grand debates of humanity about the individual and society, freedom and responsibility, the absurd and meaning. The seeming lack of connection between events and feelings, the ironies and the incongruities of the trial, portray a world in which community, God and other kinds of transcendence no longer seem credible. Yet despite the lack of meaning Meursault knows that life is worth living.

Critics often see the influence of 20th-century American literature on *The Stranger*. Camus later explained that he used the technique of such authors as Ernest Hemingway (1899–1961) and John Steinbeck (1902–1968) to describe *a man with no apparent inner life*. He felt, however, that the American novel was elementary.[67] Among his contemporaries in America he admired William Faulkner (1897–1962), from whose novel he later adapted a play, *Requiem for a Nun*. More important for Camus was Herman Melville (1819–1891), whose *Moby Dick*, with its powerful images of man fighting against the elements, would influence *The Plague*.

He was also writing *The Myth of Sisyphus*. The first part was finished by September 1940. In a letter to Claude de Fréminville, he says he wants to publish, if possible at the same time, three works on 'the Absurd': *The Stranger*, *The Myth of Sisyphus* and *Caligula*.[68] He considered these three to be the first stage in a 'work' that would absorb him for many years. As he finished chapters of *The Myth of Sisyphus*, Francine copied the manuscript by hand, as they had no typewriter.

In January 1941, Camus's job at *Paris Soir* ended and he left with Francine for Oran, where they lived until August 1942. He comments 21 February 1941, *The three absurds are now complete. Beginnings of liberty.*[69] Camus 'seems to have looked upon the completion of a particular "cycle" of works almost as a duty, and to have looked forward to a future period when he no longer felt obliged to write a particular type of book'.[70] He now felt more sure of himself. In a letter to Jean Grenier in 1941, replying to Grenier's critical comments on *The Stranger*, Camus wrote: *Even if it's bad or less good than I hoped, I know now that it is mine and I accept being judged by it.*[71]

In Oran, where Francine had a position as a teacher, Camus was largely dependent on her income and on her family, who gave up one of their apartments to the couple. He was not always happy living with Francine's family. Her mother was a formidable woman. She worked in the post office; one day she participated in a five-minute work stoppage, which de Gaulle asked all patriots to do. As a result she was suspended without pay for two months.

Right-wing parties were strong in Oran, particularly in the area where Camus lived with the Faure family. There was much anti-Semitism, especially among those of Spanish origin. Although Jews in Algeria were not required to wear the yellow star and were not sent to the concentration camps, they were forbidden to hold normal teaching jobs. One of Francine's grandmothers was Jewish and the family was proud of their Jewish heritage. Among the friends of the Faures was a family of Jewish intellectuals, the Bénichou, with whom Camus also became friends. André Bénichou was given permission to teach private classes to Jewish children, but only to five students at a time. Camus taught French to Bénichou's pupils. Soon he also had a part-time position as a teacher of French, history and geography. He went for long walks through the city with his friend Pierre Galindo, who worked for a merchant selling local produce in the Jewish quarter. While there was some shortage of food, there was not much evidence of the war in 1941.[72]

While Camus did some editorial work for Edmond Charlot, it paid little. The drama group that he had formed in Algiers before the war, the Theatre of the Team, did occasional play readings, but no productions. He was active in helping various refugees to leave Vichy Algeria for Morocco; one was Nicola Chiaromonte (1900–1966), a political refugee from Mussolini's Italy, who managed to escape to New York, where he wrote for liberal intellectual magazines such as *Partisan Review* and *The Nation*, and remained a friend of Camus throughout his life. After he finished *The Myth of Sisyphus*, Camus was working on his next novel, *The Plague*. He ordered books on the plague from friends in Algiers, particularly Emmanuel Roblès.

The themes of *The Myth of Sisyphus*, Camus' essay on

'the Absurd' – the value of physical life, a rejection of religion, the need for lucidity, and the inevitability of death – recall the life of Meursault, his awareness of physical sensations, his anger at the prison chaplain's talk of God, and his acceptance of death. The essay begins: *There is but one truly serious philosophical problem, and that is suicide. Judging whether life is or is not worth living amounts to answering the fundamental question of philosophy.* He decides that one must continue living to maintain 'the Absurd', the insoluble opposition between what man would like - a comprehensible world without death - and reality, where we all die and the world is not rational. *What is absurd is the confrontation of this irrational and the wild longing for clarity whose call echoes in the human heart. The absurd depends as much on man as on the world.* The confrontation between man and the world is a constant act of 'revolt', *the certainty of a crushing fate, without the resignation that ought to accompany it.* Since death makes a mockery of all plans, each man has the liberty of the condemned prisoner, to accumulate the greatest quantity of experiences, and to be passionately conscious of them.[73]

Camus gives several illustrations of the life of an absurd hero. The Don Juan goes from woman to woman, *it is indeed because he loves them with the same passion and each time with his whole self that he must repeat his gift and his profound quest.* The artist, if he is a writer, is *the most absurd character*. He must simply describe the absurd confrontation between man and the world, not try to explain it rationally. He must be aware, however, that no artistic fame can console him for his own death. Camus ends *The Myth of Sisyphus* with his version of the Sisyphus myth. Sisyphus was condemned by the gods to a meaningless and never-ending task.

Yet, because he was conscious, he could retain his dignity and surmount his face by scorn: *The struggle itself towards the heights is enough to fill a man's heart. One must imagine Sisyphus happy.*[74]

Camus himself was not happy in Oran as he felt too dependent on the Faure family. In letters to Jean Grenier and other friends, he wrote of his need to leave the city. He also found it impossible to be true to Francine. He wrote to Yvonne regularly, and spent a week with her, which provoked a strong reaction from Francine's sister and mother. In the autumn of 1941, he wrote to Yvonne: *I can no longer see you. Excuse me for how absurd the situation is. I am unhappy and I love you, but even that is in vain.*[75] In *The Myth of Sisyphus* Don Juan sees love not as tending towards the eternal, but as an immediate sensation, which *recognizes itself to be both short-lived and exceptional.*[76]

Pascal Pia was trying to find work for Camus in France and was also looking for a publisher for *The Stranger* and *The Myth of Sisyphus*. Among those to whom Pia sent the two finished manuscripts and who read them with great enthusiasm were the novelist André Malraux and Jean Paulhan (1884–1968), a critic, writer and editorial adviser for Gallimard. In December 1941 Gaston Gallimard (1881–1975) wrote to Camus, proposing a contract for *The Stranger*, with 10 per cent royalties on the first 10,000 copies, and an advance of 5,000 francs, an offer Camus accepted. Many anti-Nazi writers during the Occupation were uncertain about whether to publish. Camus didn't have the choice of writers with private means; he also felt that with his bad lungs he might not have many years to write. He did, however, refuse to let his novel be published in *La Nouvelle Revue Française*, Gallimard's prominent literary journal, which was under German control.

Gallimard had to submit the manuscript of *The Stranger* to the German censor, who read the book immediately and found it enthralling. There was later, however, a problem about *The Myth of Sisyphus*, as it included a chapter on the Jewish writer, Franz Kafka (1883–1924). This chapter had to be removed and replaced with an essay on Dostoevsky. Camus later published the Kafka essay separately and it was reintegrated into the book after the war.

He also had trouble with the censors about 'The Minotaur or the stop in Oran', an essay he wanted to publish in Algeria in 1942. It is an amusing, ironic look at Oran society: *how can one feel tender in a town where nothing appeals to the mind, where even ugliness is anonymous, where the past is reduced to nothing?*[77] Camus humorously describes a boxing match, mocks the architecture, comments on the rivalry between Algiers and Oran, which has no basis. Some of the descriptions of Oran as a city that has turned its back to the sea will be used in *The Plague*. The German censors refused publication, seeing the essay as an attack on local patriotism. It is, however, much less subversive towards established society than *The Stranger*.

The Stranger was published 19 May 1942. There were few papers or magazines to review novels in wartime Paris. *The Stranger* did get a favourable review in a weekly, *Comoedia*, as well as a hostile review in *Le Figaro*, and reviews, often lacking comprehension, in provincial papers. Camus commented on the criticism in his notebook: *The air is ringing with high moral principles.*[78] He was still in Oran when *The Stranger* was published, and had been in poor health since the end of January, when he had a bad coughing fit and told Francine, *I thought it was all over for me this time.*[79]

In July 1942 Camus and Francine took a ship to Marseilles,

then a train to Lyons, where Camus was too exhausted even to see Pascal Pia. The couple then travelled to Le Panelier, a small village in the Massif Central near Chambon, 1000 metres above sea level, where Camus planned to recuperate at a boarding house run by Francine's aunt. He had regular pneumothorax (collapse therapy) for his lungs in nearby Saint Etienne, continued his writing, and to relax picked mushrooms. He comments in his notebooks about his illness. In October he remarks: *My youth is fleeing from me: that is what being ill means*, and in November: *Be silent, lungs. Devour this wan and icy air, which is your food. Keep quiet. And let me cease hearing your slow decay.* Later he writes of *The sensation of death which from now on is familiar to me.*[80]

As Francine had a job as a teacher and they were in need of money, she returned to Algeria at the end of September. In November 1942 the Allied forces landed in and conquered Algeria, which then became 'enemy territory' for the Vichy government. Camus missed the last ship to return home, and was cut off from Francine for several years. She worked with the Allied forces in Oran, producing anti-Vichy propaganda. Camus did manage to write to her, indirectly, through an acquaintance in Portugal, but she was unable to send him money. He was often lonely in Le Panelier. During February 1943 he writes of *Four months of lonely and ascetic life. The will and the mind profit. But the heart?*[81] He felt he was losing self-confidence.

His life in Le Panelier is reflected in his writing. Separation from loved ones became a theme of *The Plague*. The notebooks from 1942–43 often emphasize how the plague separates families and lovers: *I want to express by means of the plague the suffocation from which we all suffered and the atmosphere of threat and exile in which we lived.*[82] Some of the people he met around Le Panelier were models for characters in the novel. He was also writing a play, which became *Le Malentendu (The Misunderstanding)*, set in a central European country, but rather like the mountainous plateau on which he was then living.

The region around Chambon had been a stronghold of French Protestantism from the 16th century. Protestants knew about persecution of minorities; Chambon became during the war a refuge for those needing to flee the German occupiers, especially many Jews. There was an active Resistance movement in the area. During his stay at Le Panelier, Camus met people who worked in the Resistance movement. René Leynaud (1910–1944), a journalist and poet with whom Camus stayed on a visit to Lyons, was assassinated by the Nazis in October 1944, a death about which Camus wrote an editorial in *Combat*: Leynaud *joined the Resistance in the first months of the war. The elements of which his moral life was composed –Christianity and truth to his word – drove him to take his place, silently, in the shadowy battle.*[83] Raymond Léopold Bruckberger (1907–1998), a Dominican priest, writer and later filmmaker, was the informal chaplain of the Resistance. With Francis Ponge (1899–1988), a poet and a Communist, from a Protestant family in the region around Chambon, Camus continued a correspondence throughout his life.

In Lyons Camus joined the Comité National des Ecrivains (National Committee of Writers), which included Communist and non-Communist writers. The Communist poet Louis Aragon (1891–1982) was head of the southern French section. Camus resigned from the CNE in late 1944 because of its overwhelming Communist orientation. Although he did not take part in any Resistance actions whilst living in Le

Panelier, he did contribute essays to underground magazines, among them letters addressed to a supposed German friend, in which he explains how he has gone beyond pacifist leanings to realize that armed resistance to the Nazis is necessary. He predicts victory soon for France, as the country is now fighting, after having gone through what he terms a 'detour' (an indirect reference to Vichy). For Camus, a belief that there is no transcendent meaning in the universe must not lead to the rejection of good and evil and the glorification of the 'mother country', but to a fight for justice, without which patriotism is meaningless. Two essays, dated July and December 1943, were published in Resistance magazines. The third and fourth essays, dated April and July 1944, were not published during the Occupation. The four essays were published in book form in 1945 as *Lettres à un ami allemand* (*Letters to a German friend*).

Pascal Pia arranged for Gallimard to put Camus on its payroll as a reader. Camus obtained a pass from the German occupiers on the 28th of December 1942 to go to Paris for two weeks, where he met Gaston Gallimard and others at the publishing company for the first time and was welcomed as *The Stranger* was selling well. In February 1943 *The Stranger* was reviewed twice in *Cahiers du Sud* (published in Marseilles), by Jean Grenier and by Sartre. Sartre's 'Explication de *L'Etranger*' (Explanation of *The Stranger*) discussed the relationship between the novel and the essay, *The Myth of Sisyphus,* which had been published in October 1942. The title might be seen as patronizing: Sartre, the professional philosopher, can explain what Camus meant. Camus commented on Sartre's review in a letter to Jean Grenier: *in any creative work there is an instinctive part which he does not consider. Intelligence does not have such a prominent role.* In his review of Sartre's *Nausea* in 1938, he had said that *theory harms life.*[84] Sartre is too much a philosopher, not an artist. The opposition between Sartre, a philosopher and Camus, whom Sartre would say was not a philosopher, would continue into the postwar years. Camus returned to Paris briefly in June 1943, when he met Sartre at the opening of Sartre's play *Les Mouches* (*The Flies*). At that time Camus showed a section of *The Plague* to Jean Paulhan, who arranged for the article to be published in *Domaine Français*, printed in Switzerland and smuggled into France.

In September 1943 Father Bruckberger invited Camus to stay in the Saint Maximin Dominican monastery in Provence, in southern France. Afterwards, Camus wrote to Ponge that he intended to stay clear of both Bruckberger's Christianity and Ponge's Marxism. Christianity gave man *a humiliated image of himself* in contrast to *the classical ideal with its admirable image of man.*[85] The rejection of any ideological system attempting to control human beings would become a major theme of Camus' second book of essays, *L'Homme révolté* (*The Rebel*).

Albert Camus at the rehearsals of *L'Etat de siège* at the Marigny Theatre in Paris in 1948. Seen with him are Jean-Louis Barrault, Pierre Brasseur, Madeleine Renaud, the artist Balthus, Arthur Honegger and at the centre of the photograph Maria Casarès.

4

November 1943–August 1945: Combat and Paris

During November 1943 Camus was able to leave Le Panelier and move to Paris to work as a reader in the Gallimard
publishing company. There he met Michel Gallimard (1918–
1960), a nephew of Gaston. Michel and his wife Janine Tho-
masset (whom Camus had met when she worked for *Paris
Soir* in 1940) became some of Camus' closest friends and
helped him financially in the early years of his career. He
would become a regular employee of Gallimard, the main
French publisher of serious literature and an editor of the
influential newspaper *Combat*.

He became friendly with Sartre, who had written his first
play *Huis Clos* (*No Exit*). He asked Camus to direct it and
to play the major male role. It was initially intended to be an
amateur production, but when a prominent theatre decided
to take it on, Camus was no longer involved, either because he
felt unable to direct professional actors or because the theatre
told Sartre to find an experienced director.[86]

Camus soon began going with Sartre and Simone de Beauvoir to restaurants, clubs and parties. At the home of Michel

Leiris (1901–1990), a noted writer and ethnologist, they gave a public reading of a play by the Spanish artist Pablo Picasso (1881–1973). From her memoirs, it is clear that Beauvoir was jealous of the attention Sartre paid Camus.

The first of Camus' plays to be produced was *The Misunderstanding*, which he had written in Le Panelier in 1942–43. It is based on a legend, but also on an incident in Belgrade in 1935. After having had a successful career in a country in the sun, a man returns to his home, a dark, depressing village in Czechoslovakia (a country where Camus himself had been depressed during his visit in 1936). He intends to help his mother and sister, but does not immediately identify himself. They kill their hotel visitors for their money, and murder him without knowing who he is. When they discover the truth, they commit suicide. The man's wife, coming to meet him, finds the dead bodies and cries out for help. The old manservant replies simply *No*. In the preface to the American edition of his plays, Camus said that the servant did not necessarily symbolize fate: *If he answers 'No' when she asks him to help her, this is because … at a certain level of suffering or injustice, no one can do anything for anyone. Pain is solitary.* The play seems bitter and nihilistic, but Camus saw a possible message: *Doubtless, it is a very dismal image of human fate. But it can be reconciled with a relative optimism as to man. For, after all, it amounts to saying that … in an unjust or indifferent world man can save himself, and save others, by practicing the most basic sincerity and pronouncing the most appropriate word.*[87]

Simone de Beauvoir (1908–1986), Sartre's companion and a major philosopher and writer, is most famous for *Le deuxième sexe* (*The Second Sex*, 1949). She described the relationship of the three intellectuals in her autobiographies, particularly *La Force des Choses* (*The Force of Circumstance*, 1963), which covers the years from 1944 to 1962.

52

This seems a more optimistic interpretation than most audiences find in the play.

At the first meeting in the theatre to discuss the play, Camus found Maria Casarès, whom he had met briefly in 1942. For both of them it was immediately a passionate attraction and Maria became the greatest love of his life. Both were obsessed with Spain and loved to dance. They became celebrities, whose entrance to a nightclub was signaled by the orchestra playing a *pase doble*.

The opening night of *The Misunderstanding* was 24 June 1944. Casarès' performance as the sister was praised, but the play itself was booed. One problem was the language, which Camus realized shocked the audience. He tried to find a language that was *natural enough to be spoken by contemporaries, yet sufficiently unusual to suggest the tragic tone*. He was unsure if he succeeded in this mixture.[88] He made some stylistic changes when *The Misunderstanding* was performed for television in 1950 and 1955. It has since become part of the classic repertoire of French theatres.

Maria Casarès (1922–1996) came from a Spanish family in exile in France. Her father was prime minister in the government of the second Spanish republic and Maria did volunteer work with the Republican wounded. After her father had been forced to resign in July 1936, Maria studied acting and was soon given roles by prominent directors. She became perhaps the greatest tragic actress in France during the later 20th century. She also acted in films, including Marcel Carné's *Children of Paradise* (1945).

He was, in theory, part of the editorial committee of *Lettres françaises* (*French Letters*), largely in the hands of Communist writers who thought that 'Camus was not hard enough'.[89] More important was his work with the *Combat* team to which Pascal Pia had introduced him towards the end of 1943. He wrote only a few articles for the underground edition, but had other jobs, including typesetting. The team were already preparing for open publication after the liberation of Paris. The editorial secretary, Jacqueline Bernard (1918–2007), of a prominent Alsatian Jewish family, organized the teams of writers, printers, and distributors. Describing what Camus did, Bernard said that he played 'a decisive role at a time when every meeting and every initiative held great risks'.[90] He did not, however, according to a letter he wrote in 1949, handle any arms.[91] The first issue of *Combat* published clandestinely from Paris was probably No. 49 (15 October 1943).

The atmosphere in Paris after the Allied landing in Normandy on D Day (6 June 1944) was tense. Camus and Casarès were stopped in a police roundup when he was carrying an incriminating document for *Combat*. He narrowly escaped by passing the document to Casarès, as women were not always thoroughly searched.[92] Camus sometimes had to hide out of Paris. When the police arrived at the workshop of *Combat* on 17 June 1944, the printer, André Bollier (1920–1944) committed suicide rather than risk informing on the network. Jacqueline Bernard was trapped by an informer on 11 July 1944, and arrested. She managed to warn her comrades, before being sent to a camp. (The Germans did not realize that she was Jewish. After the war she worked with Camus at *Combat*.)

With the liberation of Paris on 21 August 1944, *Combat* began publishing openly with issue No. 59 (as the clandestine issues for the past three years were counted). Pascal Pia was the director, and Camus was the editor in chief. After his arrival from England on 26 August de Gaulle closed the newspapers that had published during the German occupation. *Combat* took over the premises of a collaborationist newspaper. New papers were allotted a number of copies they could print. *L'Humanité*, the Communist daily, was allotted 300,000 copies and *Combat* 180,000 copies.

Camus suddenly gained a readership of thousands and became a famous journalist. His opinions were widely cited and, to his chagrin, he was often considered a moral mentor. He was well aware of the problems of journalism: *A profession that involves daily judgment of breaking news ... is not without dangers... . In this business, it is but one step from the presumptuous to the foolish.*[93] His health was not good; even on the day Paris was liberated, he went to the doctor for pneumothorax injections.[94] When the American president Franklin Delano Roosevelt (1882–12 April 1945) died, Camus, perhaps thinking of his own poor health, praised Roosevelt's fortitude: *he knew one thing: that there is no pain that cannot be overcome with energetic and conscientious effort.*[95]

Although Camus had energy, his life was complicated. As well as working on his second novel, he was a reader at Gallimard, editor of a daily newspaper, lover of Maria Casarès and husband of a wife who arrived from Algeria in October 1944 to live with him. He had been able to rent an apartment from André Gide through Gide's connection with the Gallimards. Camus paid directly, without official documents, so the police would not have his address, but also so that Gide would not have to pay taxes on the rent. Francine's sister Christiane, who arrived before Francine, was quickly aware of the situation between Camus and Casarès. Camus told Casarès that Francine was like a sister, but when Francine became pregnant, Casarès broke off the relationship.[96]

The editorial work at *Combat* was time-consuming but satisfying. Camus enjoyed working with the printers, as he had for *Paris Soir* in Lyon. His camaraderie with co-workers, as with the team when he played football, was the most satisfying part of his life. He was not a typical Parisian intellectual. He was, however, typical of his generation in his insistence on 'virile' behaviour. In his biography of Camus Olivier Todd finds latent sexism in Camus' language in *Combat*. Catherine Camus, his daughter, agreed that her father was 'sexist'.[97] A psychiatrist friend who met Camus later commented that he 'always took it for granted that he, and not a woman, would go through a door first'.[98] The macho attitude is evident in *The First Man*, where the father, explaining why the child is born rather quickly after the family's arrival in a new town, explains that *he had been expecting the event later and that he must have made a mistake*,[99] oddly attributing calculation of the birth date to the man rather than the woman.

In the first years Camus wrote over 150 articles for *Combat*. He usually dictated them from notes to a secretary, and had little time to revise. He found that the pressure of writing on current events stimulated his reflections on universal themes.[100] He cultivated a rhetorical style: *Paris is firing all its ammunition into the August night. Against a vast backdrop of water and stone, on both sides of a river awash with history, freedom's barricades are once again being erected.* Or: *A great nation is one that rises to confront its own tragedies…. We must do everything at once or accomplish nothing at all.*[101]

Combat's policy was to reject ideologies: *We do not believe in ready-made principles or theoretical plans.*[102] The paper supported the socialists in October 1945 in the election for the Constituent Assembly to form a new government, but only as the least bad choice. Camus was often naive in some of his political opinions, still believing in 1944 that the Russian people supported their government. He welcomed talks between de Gaulle and Stalin, and felt it was necessary to give Russia *the place she has earned with her superhuman sacrifices*. In 1945 he felt that the French Communist Party was *well suited to take charge of the ministry of national economy*. He supported *a collectivist economy*, and approved of de Gaulle's decision to put electricity and coal into the hands of the national government. He was also somewhat naive and vague on economic policies. Discussion of the food crisis in the winter of 1944 in Paris, led him to attack expensive restaurants.[103]

Among the subjects of editorials in the first years of *Combat* were the need for morality in journalism, the need to reform socialism, and the need to preserve the spirit of the Resistance. His experiences during the war led him to question the individualism of his 'absurd' period. The ideas of *The Myth of Sisyphus* had to be considered because *our generation has encountered them and must learn to live with them.*[104] Without denying his earlier work, however, he was developing a new ethic of man's responsibility for his fellow beings.

On international themes, Camus criticized the Allied acceptance of Franco's government in Spain. He thought that the Allied powers should recognize the provisional French government. (France was not present at several major conferences in October 1944, where the groundwork for international institutions was laid.) *Combat* called for a world economic federation and was critical of the new United Nations. The veto by the members of the Security Council would, Camus felt, *effectively put an end to any idea of international democracy.*[105]

The purge of those who had collaborated with the German occupiers posed difficult issues. In France demands for the execution of writers who had helped the Nazis were louder than demands for execution of industrialists and bankers (perhaps an indication of the importance intellectuals have long held in French culture, perhaps simply an indication of the power of money to avert judgment). Camus had been against the death penalty since his youth, but, when he thought of those he knew, such as René Leynaud, did not exclude death for collaboration. He became engaged in a long debate with the Catholic novelist François Mauriac (1885–1970), Mauriac advocating Christian charity, Camus human justice: *we must renounce that part of ourselves that would prefer the consolations of forgetfulness and tenderness. Four years ago we were forced to harden some parts of ourselves.*[106] He calls, however, for prompt justice; all prosecution for crimes should end at a fixed date, after which lesser acts of collaboration should be consigned to oblivion. The case of Robert Brasillach (1909–1945), a writer and journalist condemned to death for his collaboration, was particularly difficult for Camus. Many intellectuals signed a petition asking for grace for Brasillach. After much hesitation, Camus signed the petition, because of his growing aversion to the death penalty, but added a letter to de Gaulle stating how much he scorned Brasillach. De Gaulle refused clemency.

During this period, Camus reflected on violence, which he saw as a necessity during the war. Gradually he became disillusioned with what seemed politics as usual, and particularly with the purge, writing of the *absurd sentences and preposterous instances of leniency*. He could not, however, believe in pardons, stating that only the families of those who had died under torture could pardon the torturers. He was slowly moving towards a refusal of any capital punishment, even for Philippe Pétain, head of the Vichy government, who had collaborated with Hitler: *every death sentence is an affront to morality.*[107]

Later, in a speech at the Dominican monastery of Latour-Mauberg in 1946, Camus said that Mauriac was right: *the fever of those years, the painful memories of my murdered friends, are what led me to the position I took. I can say here that, despite some excessively harsh language on the part of François Mauriac, I have never stopped thinking about what he said. ... I have come to admit to myself and to admit publicly here that on the central issue of our argument, M. Mauriac was right and I was wrong.*[108]

In his articles and editorials on France's colonial empire, Camus advocates freedom and justice for the colonies, without directly considering their independence. Occasionally he writes about Indochina, but his main interest is Algeria. He is critical of the French Algerian population: *much of this population supported the policies of Vichy... . the colonial spirit has always resisted innovation of any kind, even when the most elementary sense of justice demanded it.* He often writes of his respect for the 'Arab' people, *a people of impressive traditions ... not inferior except in regard to the conditions in which they must live.*[109]

Messali Hadj (1898–1974) was secretary-general of the Etoile nord-africaine (North African Star), a movement to fight for the rights of North Africans in France and in North Africa. In 1927 he was the first to call for Algerian independence. In 1936, when he returned to Algeria from France, he rejected assimilation. The ENA was outlawed and Hadj spent years in prison and under house arrest. In 1946 he founded the Movement for the Triumph of Democratic Liberties (MTLD). Younger activists deserted Hadj's movement, which was pragmatic and moderate, for the National Liberation Front (FLN). In 1958 he urged compromise between Algerians and the French, but his effectiveness was over.

Camus went to Algeria in April 1945, to write a series of articles for *Combat* on the politics and economy of the colony. He had not anticipated what would be happening there. A radical leader, Messali Hadj, who advocated independence, was sent into exile by the French authorities on 25 April. Protesters at May Day celebrations in several towns demanded his return. Riots broke out in Sétif and Guelma on 8 May (perhaps incidentally the day Germany surrendered). The French authorities claimed 103 Europeans were killed, many wounded, some raped. In the repression thousands of Muslims (perhaps as many as 6–10,000) were shot.

Camus' articles do not address the riots, which he did not witness. His main concern was to show the faults of the colonial administration, which had rejected the Blum-Violette laws and which had allowed famine to develop; the riots having been, he felt, the main cause of this. Grain was not being distributed equally, as the European population received much more. He wrote of the Algerian soldiers who fought in the war: *People who have not been stingy with their blood in this war are justified in thinking that others should not be stingy with their bread.* He also called for a programme of extending rights to Muslims and of an egalitarian social policy, a programme that was *France's last chance to safeguard its future in North Africa.* France has waited too long, and missed the opportunity to make assimilation accessible. The days of Western imperialism are over.[110]

Ferhat Abbas (1889–1985) in the late 1930s had defended a policy of assimilation. He was falsely blamed for the Sétif riots in 1945 and imprisoned. At that time he probably met Camus, with whose positions he was in sympathy. By 1954, Abbas decided that the condition of the Algerians could not be changed through legal means. In May 1955 he joined the FLN, the movement for Algerian independence and separation from France, founded in 1954. He was the first president of the provisional government founded by the FLN in 1958 and one of the leaders of Algerian nationalism. After Algerian independence, he was president of the first Algerian Constituent Assembly. He resigned later, having criticized the 'fascist' tendencies of the government and retired from public life.

He describes the policies of the more moderate Muslim leader, Ferhat Abbas, who had earlier advocated assimilation and who was still willing to accept a legislature with 50 per cent Europeans, 50 per cent Muslims, even though there were eight Muslims to every Frenchman. Camus refrains from trying to choose between assimilation and Abbas's call for *Algeria to be recognized as a nation linked to France by ties of federalism*. He concludes that *Only the infinite power of justice can help us reconquer Algeria and its people*.[111]

When the first atomic bomb was dropped on Hiroshima 8 August 1945, Camus was the only French journalist to express his horror. While hoping that the bomb would lead to Japan's surrender, he felt: *the civilization of the machine has just achieved its ultimate degree of savagery. A choice is going to have to be made in the fairly near future, between collective suicide and the intelligent utilization of scientific discoveries*. It was, as Jean Daniel later commented to Camus, a brave decision, going against the opinion of people he admired.[112]

Pia and Camus had high standards for *Combat*, which was built on the work of many who had risked their lives for the paper during the war. There were to be no 'Letters to the Editor' and definitely no horoscopes (still a regular feature of supposedly 'cultural' newspapers in France). Camus had a moralizing tone, which exasperated other journalists, but which established an ethical standard not reached by most newspapers. He criticized popular journalism that contained *appeals to the shopgirl sensibility that filled the columns of our papers before and after the war*. Of an article about the arrival in Metz of Marlene Dietrich (1901–1992), the German-American film star, he commented: *we don't think that the doings of movie stars are necessarily of greater interest than the suffering of peoples*.[113]

Camus became increasingly less enthusiastic about the possibility of achieving a new social order in France. He was particularly depressed by the failure of the postwar purge, and by the return of many of the people and policies of the Third Republic of the 1930s. Primarily because of exhaustion and ill health, he wrote no editorials for *Combat* from 17 February to 9 March 1945 and by summer he took a year's leave to work on *The Plague*, the novel he had started in Le Panelier, but which was going very slowly.

Camus photographed while making a broadcast in 1948.

5

September 1945–1947: *Caligula* and *The Plague*

After the Second World War ended, Camus often felt isolated politically, neither at home with the Communist Left
under the leadership of Maurice Thorez, or the Gaullist
Right. He was especially discouraged by the failure to create
a free press that could compete financially with the popular
newspapers. He took a year's absence from *Combat* to work
on *The Plague* but he remained active at Gallimard. He was
a member of the editorial committee and soon the editor
of a series, *L'Espoir* (*Hope*), which published fiction and
non-fiction, including a posthumous work by Simone Veil
(1909–1943), *L'Enracinement* (*The Need for Roots*), focusing
on her search for social justice and for non-violence, a search
that paralleled his own thought. He published 24 titles in the
Hope series. As an editor at Gallimard he read many manuscripts, received as many as 100 letters a week and wrote
polite rejection letters. *To ensure my freedom to work as a
writer,* a second profession was necessary.[114]

Originally outlined in a note as far back as January 1937
and revised frequently, *Caligula* was the first play that Camus

wrote. Based on his reading of *The Lives of Twelve Caesars* by the Roman historian Suetonius (about 70–128 AD), his Caligula is a flamboyant young emperor who reacts violently to his discovery of 'absurdity': *'Men die and they are not happy'*. As the Roman patricians have refused to face this reality, Caligula decides to force them to recognize the lack of meaning in the world by acting in an irrational manner. The play is a series of tableaux illustrating how he destroys the moral values of the patricians, their personal integrity and their belief in reason. He forces the families of victims to laugh, capriciously kills men, arbitrarily closes the country's granaries and declares a famine. Just before he is killed in a patrician uprising, he realizes that he has chosen the wrong way: *killing is not the solution … Yet who can condemn me in this world where there is no judge, where nobody is innocent*. In the preface to his plays, Camus wrote that if Caligula's *truth is to rebel against fate, his error lies in negating what binds him to mankind*.[115]

Charles de Gaulle (1890–1970), who fled to England in 1940, and led the Resistance movement during the war from there, was president of the provisional French government from 1944 to 20 January 1946, when he retired as a protest against the constitution of the Fourth Republic. In April 1947 he created a new movement, the *Rassemblement du Peuple Français* (the Union of the French People, the RPF). He would return to power in 1958, during the Algerian crisis. Maurice Thorez (1900–1964) was the general secretary of the French Communist Party from 1930 until his death. He left the army as a deserter for Russia in 1940, but as a Communist leader was counted a 'resistance fighter' after the war. He negotiated his return and his participation in the provisional government where from 1945 to 1947 he held ministerial posts.

Camus attended auditions in August, and selected a young actor, Gérard Philippe (1922–1959) for the part of the emperor Caligula. It was the start of Philippe's career; he became the most sought-after actor in postwar Paris. The director of the play was Paul Oettly (the son of the woman who had housed Camus in Le Panelier, and a relative of Francine). Oettly (1890–1959) went on to become a well-known film actor. Several friends from Camus' days with the Team Theatre in Algiers worked on the play, which opened on 26 September 1945. While there were many reviews, Camus noted: *Thirty articles. Praised and blamed for equally bad reasons. Fame! In the best of cases, a misunderstanding. But I shall not adopt the superior air of the man who disdains it.*[116]

He was a father by the time the play opened. Francine gave birth to twins, Jean and Catherine, 5 September 1945. She later told friends that her husband got into the car, and was ready to leave the hospital, forgetting about the babies. He gradually became used to having children around, and was a good father, singing Spanish songs to the infants. They of course cried, which made it hard for him to work, and he envied Sartre and de Beauvoir for their freer life. The family moved several times, finding accommodation with the help of the Gallimards. They later had an apartment in a renovated mansion, where the ceilings were very high in proportion to the small rooms. This is the very apartment that Camus described with humour in 'Jonas or the Artist at Work', published in *Exile and the Kingdom*: *some very modern arrangements had given it an original character that consisted chiefly of offering its residents a great volume of air while occupying only a limited surface.* In this apartment the artist, Jonas, tried to work in a cramped space as his wife *produced two children in quick succession, a boy and a girl.*[117]

Jean-Paul Sartre, Camus and Simone de Beauvoir had a regularly scheduled lunch once a week, and saw each other at the literary cafés around Saint German de Près and at various nightclubs. Both Sartre and Camus liked to dance. Camus was, however, better looking and more successful with women, which Sartre resented. When he had been drinking, Sartre 'would begin to boast about how handsome he was, and often he'd become belligerent'. Simone de Beauvoir was interested in Camus, but he avoided her 'because he feared she would talk too much in bed'.[118] Camus told a friend years later that de Beauvoir came to his office once to tell him that a friend of hers wanted to sleep with him. He replied that he made his own choices; she felt humiliated and did not forget it.[119]

In July 1945 Sartre published a flattering essay about Camus in the American edition of *Vogue*. Politically, however, the two were growing apart. To Sartre, Communist parties were the incarnation of the proletariat; the USSR must always be supported against the USA. Simone de Beauvoir noted in her journal that Camus defended de Gaulle against Maurice Thorez. In October 1945 Camus published 'Remarque sur la révolte' ('Note on rebellion'), in an anthology edited by Jean Grenier; it was a draft of the first chapter of *The Rebel* (1951), the essay that would mark the complete break between the two men.

Camus questioned Christianity as well as Communism. He wrote to a Catholic student in Belgium about his own search for values without a belief in God. Man does not need the eternal but must find *another road … without too much pride and without too many illusions.*[120] *If Christianity is pessimistic as to man, it is optimistic as to human destiny. Well, I can say that, pessimistic as to human destiny, I am optimistic as to man.*[121] Many Catholic priests respected Camus and kept hoping to convert him. In 1946, at the Dominican Monastery in Latour-Maubourg, Camus gave a talk, 'The

Unbeliever and Christians'. His criticisms are addressed to what the Church and Christians do, more than to what they believe. He condemns the Spanish bishop who blesses political executions as not a Christian or even a man. Christians should, however, be able to join with others to intercede for the rights of man. In Stockholm in 1957 Camus would reply to a question about religion: *I respect and venerate the person of Christ and his story. I do not believe in his resurrection.*[122]

In 1946 Camus went on a tour to the United States, under the sponsorship of the Cultural Relations Section of the French Ministry of Foreign Affairs. On arrival at American immigration on the 25th of March 1946 he had a problem as he refused to identify friends as Communist. He had stated on his visa application that he had never been a member of the Communist Party, presumably a necessary lie to enter the United States. The FBI had opened a file on Camus, an 'existentialist', associated with *Combat*, whose slogan was 'From the Resistance to the Revolution'. The investigation led to nothing but confusion for the investigators.

Camus spoke to groups at several universities, usually in French, with a translator. (He had a good reading knowledge of English but was very limited in speaking.) At Columbia University, he spoke to 1,200 on the 'Crisis of Mankind'. Among his stories for the lecture was an incident he had recorded earlier in his notebooks: *The concierge of the Gestapo, who took over two floors of a building in the rue de la Pompe. In the morning, she cleans up with the tortured bodies all around. 'I never bother with what my tenants do.'*[123] Camus continued by invoking the need to go beyond feeling that everything is meaningless and that History (in the Marxist sense of the dialectical process towards the future when the proletariat will rule) justifies any values. As the United Nations was soon to meet in New York, Camus used this lecture as an opportunity to declare that after the Nuremberg trials capital punishment should be banned internationally. While he was speaking someone stole the box office receipts, which were supposed to go to a fund for French children. When the theft was discovered, everyone agreed to pay again, much to the fund's benefit: *Everyone gives much more and the receipts are considerable. Typical of American generosity.*[124]

Camus was interviewed for several American publications, including *The New Yorker* and *Vogue.* The interview pages included photographs of him, and he was said to look like a young Humphrey Bogart. He found that although the United States was a strong and free country, it was *'ignorant of many things, first of all, Europe.* The United States was also, of course, during the difficult European post-war years, a source of plenty. Camus sent a package of over 160 pounds of flour, sugar, coffee, baby food, tinned meat and soap back to his family in France.[125]

While he also spoke at other eastern American colleges, including Vassar and Bryn Mawr, and took a trip to French Canada, New York remained the centre of Camus's activity in America, as he was fascinated by the city. He fell in love with a young American student, Patricia Blake, who was then working for several publications, including *Vogue*, was fluent in French, and beautiful. Although at the time Camus fell ill frequently, the couple spent a few idyllic weeks together. He continued to correspond with her after he returned to France in late June, giving her advice on her career. (Patricia Blake was later a writer, associate editor of *Time* magazine, and editor of several anthologies of Russian literature.)

Camus kept a diary of his visit to America, without mentioning Patricia, or even the colleges at which he spoke. Many of his remarks about America were typical of French intellectuals of the time. He commented on Americans: according to him they looked like characters in B-films, had bad taste in neckties, were unaware of the war, shared both *anti-Semitism and the love of animals*. Like other French visitors to New York, he went to African-American clubs, admired a black pianist, and it was his *impression that only the Negroes give life, passion, and nostalgia to this country which, in their own way, they colonized*. He admitted, however: *I am out of my depth when I think of New York*.[126]

Although still in a precarious position financially, and dependent partly on his friends Michel and Janine Gallimard for housing, Camus was now a celebrity. While he was in the United States, Francine hired a maid to help with the children. When a friend came to dinner, he quickly identified the 'maid' as a reporter in disguise; she was fired immediately. (In 1954 Simone de Beauvoir used this incident in her novel *The Mandarins*, attributing it to the character representing Sartre, rather than Camus.)

On his return from New York, Camus was confronted with problems at *Combat*, where the unity of the Resistance movement had been replaced by disagreements between the Left, dominated by the Communists, and the Gaullists. Raymond Aron (1905–1983), who had been in London with de Gaulle and was sceptical of Marxism, had begun writing editorials for the paper. Aron's presence disturbed some of the staff. Camus was not working regularly with the paper, but after the first elections to the French legislature in the new Fourth Republic he contributed an important series of eight articles, 'Ni Victimes ni Bourreaux' ('Neither Victims nor Executioners'), from 19 to 30 November 1946. These articles were republished in Jean Daniel's *Caliban* magazine in

1947 and again in Camus's first collected essays, *Actuelles* ('Contemporary articles') in 1950; they are the only essays for *Combat* which have been copyrighted in his name. He wrote against the division of the world into hostile blocks and the descent of the 'iron curtain'. He felt that the 20th century was the *century of fear, lethal ideologies*, where dialogue is no longer possible. He seeks a philosophy free of *messianic elements and devoid of any nostalgia for an earthly paradise*. He cannot accept *philosophies that take history as an absolute*. The end can never justify the means. Nor can he accept a truth that might oblige him *to condemn a man to death*.[127] Emmanuel d'Astier de la Vigerie (1900–1969), an ally of both the Gaullists and the Communists, attacked 'Neither Victims nor Executioners', calling Camus a 'lay saint', an unwitting accomplice of capitalism. For Astier the end can sometimes necessitate immoral means.[128]

In 'Neither Victims nor Executioners', replying to those who say his position is utopian, Camus writes about the need to have a *relative utopia*, in which liberty, justice, and peace can only be achieved through international government, not a United Nations governed by countries with veto power. He comments with premonitory clarity on the need for a genuine internationalism: *The clash of empires is already close to taking a back seat to the clash of civilizations. Indeed, colonized civilizations from the four corners of the earth are making their voices heard. Ten or fifty years from now, the challenge will be to the preeminence of western civilization. It would therefore be better to anticipate this by opening the World Parliament to these civilizations.*[129]

He mocks those, like Sartre, who refuse to criticize the Soviet Union: *You must not talk about the purge of artists in Russia, because that would play into the hands of the reactionaries*.[130] He was more in tune with the ideas of Arthur Koestler, whom he met when Koestler came to Paris in October 1946. After the philosopher Maurice Merleau-Ponty (1908–1961), an associate of Sartre, wrote critically of Koestler, Camus accused Merleau-Ponty of trying to justify the purges in the Soviet Union. Sartre sided with Merleau-Ponty and would not speak to Camus for several months.

If he often tried to balance criticism of the Soviet Union with criticism of the West, Camus 'no longer believed, as he had perhaps once done, that the sins of the West were the equal of those of the East'.[131] He describes in his notebook a discussion with Sartre, Malraux and Koestler on 29 October 1946: *Don't you think that we are all responsible for the absence of values? And that if all of us who are the descendants of Nietzcheanism, of nihilism or of historical realism were to proclaim publicly that we were wrong and that there are moral values ... don't you think it would be the beginning of a hope? S: 'I can't turn my moral values solely against the USSR'*.[132]

Arthur Koestler (1905–1983), of Hungarian origin, had been interned in Franco's prisons during the Spanish Civil War, then joined the Communists in Germany. He broke with the Communist Party after the purges in the 1930s. A Jewish refugee from Hitler's Germany, he moved to London and began to write in English. His most famous novel, *Darkness at Noon* (1941), portrays the world of Soviet tyranny.

Koestler and his wife, Mamaine, spent many drunken evenings with Sartre and Beauvoir, and Albert and Francine Camus. Mamaine found Camus attractive, and felt that he was not deeply attached to his wife. She accepted his invitation to spend a week with him in Avignon, before she and Koestler returned to London. Camus had respect for Francine, but did not feel passionate about her. He thought her indecisive, needing his advice on many matters. He also

73

resented her family, especially her mother, who had come to Paris for the birth of the twins, and came back in July 1947. Olivier Todd, in his biography, considers several explanations for Camus's 'Don Juanism'. Did he go from woman to woman as a way of fighting a fear of illness and of death? Was he seeking the richness of existence, as he said in *The Myth of Sisyphus*? He had a number of women, many of them foreign, but 'with those he loved with passion, he went from love to affection, remaining tender towards them'.[133] Tender, perhaps, but nevertheless a misogynist. In his notebook he wrote: *outside love, women are boring. They don't know. You must live with one and be silent. Or sleep with them all and act. What is most important lies elsewhere.*[134]

Although there were a number of women, and a number of nights partying, Camus always felt the need to work, to fulfil his plans. He notes that he must make a continual effort in order to create: *It has taken me years of perseverance to escape from amusements*. He also felt that his memory was going, and that he must write more in his notebooks, even what is *personal*. Although he was always reticent about describing his private life, he was probably already planning to prepare the notebooks for publication.[135]

As the paper was losing money, the staff of *Combat* held discussions about how to survive. There were various take-over offers, including one to make *Combat* the newspaper of the Gaullist movement. Pascal Pia thought it would be better to stop publication, but Camus among others wanted to keep it alive. Pia, who had worked without stop on the paper, perhaps resented Camus' frequent absences. In addition to disputes about how to solve the financial crisis, there was a difference in political beliefs. Pia leaned towards supporting General de Gaulle. Eventually, there was a complete break between the two men, difficult to understand as Pia had been a supporter of Camus since they worked together on the *Alger Républicain* and had helped Camus find work in France and even a publisher for *The Stranger*. The two never spoke again. In 1948, Pia wrote an article attacking Camus's pacifism.[136]

After Pia left *Combat* Camus was editor in chief from 17 March to 3 June 1947. During those six weeks he published only six editorials and two articles; they reflect his disillusionment with the political situation in post-war France and also his exalted concept of journalism. In an editorial of 30 April 1947, he wrote: *Wheeling, dealing and chicanery are about to resume.*[137] When de Gaulle created the Union of the French People in April 1947, Camus wrote that it should be considered like any other political party, and not given preferential treatment. He attacks racist attitudes towards the Malagasy and the Arabs, and the use of torture in Madagascar, and continues his plea for a genuine international government. He is aware that France no longer possesses much power. The urgent problems are those that bear on the relations between Russia and America.[138]

In June the editorial staff turned over shares in the paper to Claude Bourdet (1909–1996), an early founder of the underground *Combat*, who had been arrested and deported. Camus resigned, as he could not give complete support to the new editor. *Combat* was later sold to a Tunisian businessman, who fired Bourdet; the newspaper was no longer a voice of those who had been in the Resistance.

Camus had been working on *The Plague* for at least five years. Patricia Blake had typed some pages for him in New York, not the first time a lover had also been a secretary! 'In addition to revising the general plan of *The Plague*, he also subjected the final manuscript to the minutest revision: it contains some 1500 variant readings.'[139] Although he wrote in his notebooks, *In all my life, never such a feeling of failure. I am not even sure that I shall finish it,*[140] he did complete the manuscript in September 1946.

The Plague was published on the 10th of June 1947, with a print-run of 100,000 copies, and soon awarded the Prix des Critiques. It concerns an epidemic that supposedly struck Oran in western Algeria sometime in the 1940s. The novel reproduces a feeling of the monotony and routine of life in a city, which, when the death rate from the plague rises, is sealed off from the outside world. There is no plot structure beyond a cycle of normality - plague - return to normality. *The Plague* recounts a struggle between the epidemic and the community, between a destructive force and a suffering group of men. The story is told by Dr Rieux, who does not identify himself as the narrator until the final pages and who does not consider himself a hero. After nine months the community returns to normal. Those who have fought the plague do not know whether they have won a victory or merely benefited from chance. Rieux realizes that the plague may return, that it can never be defeated: *the plague bacillus never dies or disappears for good; ... perhaps the day would come when, for the bane and the enlightening of men, it roused up its rats again and sent them forth to die in a happy city.*[141]

Rieux's 'chronicle' tells several interrelated stories of a group of men (*The Plague* describes a world almost without women) caught in Oran. Among them is Rambert, a journalist who came from Paris for another purpose and is unable to leave. He is separated from his loved one, and decides to help Rieux. His experience seems based partly on Camus's own separation from his wife during the war. Another of the characters is Tarrou, whose awareness of the absurdity of the world results from hearing his father plead for the death sentence of a criminal. Tarrou becomes a political revolutionary, then realizes that revolutions also use violence. Since all men carry within themselves the germ of the plague, a desire for violence, the most he can do is to limit the damage. Tarrou's story indirectly reflects Meursault's father's revulsion at capital punishment. Father Paneloux, a character based partly on Father Bruckberger, whom Camus had met in Le Panelier, and who fought in the Resistance, preaches at first that the plague is God's vengeance for man's sins. After watching innocent children die, he changes his views. For him, death and suffering are incomprehensible. If God seems neither just nor good, as man can understand Him, man must make a leap of faith. Rieux writes that none of these men is a 'hero'. If there is a hero it is Joseph Grand, a simple man, a clerk in a municipal office whose wife left him. Grand, who tries to write a novel but never gets beyond the first sentence, works with Rieux without posing any questions. In an ironic echo of *The Stranger* Meursault is linked to Cottard, a blackmailer sought by the police, who is happier during the epidemic. Cottard becomes agitated by a conversation about *a murder case which had created some stir in Algiers. A young commercial employee had killed an Algerian on a beach.*[142]

The Plague is initially about a natural phenomenon, the presence of disease and death. It recalls the Oran Camus knew in 1941 as he began the book, at a time when typhus caused thousands of deaths. The wife of his friend Emmanuel Roblès contracted the disease; a village was cordoned off by the authorities. Camus himself had a bad attack of tuberculosis at that time. While food was not readily available, the war was not much in evidence; theatres and cinemas had full programmes.[143] The plague is also a symbol of the suffering of the French people during the war. Is the choice of a natural disaster to symbolize war perpetrated by human beings a refusal to consider man's guilt? For some readers Camus's novel reflected a utopian position. This criticism would be repeated particularly by the pro-Communist Left, but also by others, such as Professor Philip Thody. Camus did not consider that because the Germans executed innocent hostages, 'the Resistance fighter risked having the death of 15 or 20 people executed as a direct result of his act of sabotage', on his conscience.[144]

Camus did not call either *The Stranger* or *The Plague* a novel. *The Plague*, especially, is not realistic. Oran is portrayed not as a particular city but as an almost mythic entity; there is no mention of either the Jews or the Arabs. In 1950 Camus noted: *My work during the first two cycles: people without lies, consequently not real… . This is why up to now I have doubtless not been a novelist in the usual meaning of the world, but rather an artist who creates myths on the scale of his passion and anguish.*[145] In 1958 he commented: *I've learned less about people, since their destiny interests me more than their reactions.* In a reply to criticism of *The Plague* as being unrealistic, he wrote: *I do not believe in realism in art.* The myth he created was, he added, clearly seen by readers to refer to the Nazis, although it was not realistic.[146]

Myths were also a way of avoiding the personal: *my whole effort has been in fact to depersonalize myself … Afterwards, I shall be able to speak in my own name.*[147] When an interviewer asks why, although Gide was a model for him, Camus never talks about his own life, Camus ignores the question. He is always reticent about his personal life in his writing. *No man has ever dared describe himself as he is.*[148]

During the years immediately following the Second World War, as French intellectuals often felt pressure to choose sides in the developing Cold War between the United States and the Soviet Union, Camus was constantly searching for a third way. In October 1947 a petition, signed by both Camus and Sartre, and a number of other intellectuals, called for European economic unity and neutrality in politics and military programmes. Almost immediately, one of Sartre's associates refused to publish the petition. In 1948 some socialists formed another party, the Rassemblement démocratique révolutionnaire (Revolutionary Democratic Union, the RDR), again refusing adherence to either the Soviet or the American bloc. Camus did not join, but supported RDR ideas. With Sartre he spoke at a final meeting of the RDR 13 December 1948. The movement was always a bit nebulous. It had no answer to the strikes in France, or to Soviet blocking of the air corridors to Berlin. With no realistic ideas, no popular support and no money, the RDR soon folded.

A different approach to world unity and peace was that of Garry Davis (1921–), an activist who created the first 'World Passport'. Davis renounced his American citizenship in Paris in 1948 and tore up his passport. His support committee in France included Camus, Gide and the Abbé Pierre (1912–2007), a French priest who fought in the Resistance and spent his life defending the poor and the marginal. Camus did not, however, naively encourage French citizens to tear up their passports. Replying to François Mauriac's criticism of his defence of Davis, Camus wrote that Davis, *has said what everyone thinks, that the only organization charged with preserving world peace is paralyzed by unbending sovereignties. …He has also shown every international organization of the present or future what the true goal of a League of Nations should be. That is all, but it is a great deal, and that is what we believed merited our support.*[149] Support for Davis was seen by Camus' critics as an echo of his naive idealism, his tendency to be vague and noble. (Davis later continued his movement, running for mayor of Washington D.C. in 1986, and for president of the United States in 2004.)

Albert Camus and René Char photographed in Provence at Isle–sur-Sorgue.

6
1947–1951: Politics and theatre after the war

Camus often expressed doubts about his writing. In an entry in his notebooks in 1947 he wrote: *after a week of loneliness, once again intense awareness of my inadequacy for the work that I began with the craziest of ambitions. Temptation to give it up... . But what am I to do? I should die without this.* He continued to set down various plans. The cycle of Revolt would include *The Plague, The Rebel* and a play (later named *The Just Assassins*). This would be followed by Judgment (*The First Man*), Love torn apart, then *Creation corrected or The System*, which would include a *great novel + great meditation + unperformable play*. By September 1948, he notes: *I have almost completed the series of works that I intended to write ten years ago. They have brought me to the point where I know my trade.*[150] Does the continual planning of his writing career perhaps reflect Camus' need to organize and discipline himself (as he often mentioned his natural tendency to be undisciplined)? Or is it a result of his undertaking a career so far removed from what he could have imagined as a child in an illiterate family? Jean Grenier, his old philosophy teacher from the University of Algiers, wrote of Camus' 'desire for greatness'.[151]

Although he gave up editing *Combat* in 1947, he continued to write articles on subjects of interest to him, including the long-term effects of the first atomic bomb, the French suppression of revolt in Madagascar, the Soviet invasion of Hungary, the admission of Franco's Spain to UNESCO, capital punishment. Largely because of his journalism, Camus was often thought to be a moral mentor by his readers, a position that he found disagreeable. He scorned the idea that he could tell anyone how to live.

Nor did he appreciate critics who did not see that his work had evolved since *The Stranger* and *The Myth of Sisyphus*. In an essay written in 1950, 'The Enigma', he writes: *people insist I identify my term or terms, once and for all. To make a name in literature, therefore, it is no longer indispensable to write books. It is enough to be thought of as having written one which the evening papers will have mentioned and which one can fall back on for the rest of one's life*. Camus was always unhappy with the Parisian intellectual world, which he compared to those who lived in Plato's cave, who mistake shadows for truth: *Paris is a wondrous cave, and its inhabitants, seeing their own shadows reflected on the far wall, take them for the only reality there is.*[152] A trip to Algeria was a way of forgetting about Paris. In 1947 he wrote 'A Short Guide to Towns without a Past', about what he loved: beaches, the sun, the beauty of the young people. (By 'young people' he means the French of Algeria, which he calls *a bastard race*. There is no mention of the Arab population.)[153]

Camus had published René Char in his series *Hope*, for Gallimard. In the autumn of 1947, he went to Char's home on L'Isle-sur-la-Sorgue, and brought his mother from Algeria for a holiday. Char and Camus became close friends. In *Combat* 14 March 1949, Camus and Char co-signed a letter protesting the condemnation to death of two Algerian soldiers for desertion during the Second World War. Camus later learned that the death sentences were not carried out.[154] In 1951 Char wrote to Camus: 'I think that our brotherhood – on all levels – will last longer than we might think… Our new fight begins, and our reason to exist.'[155]

After his visit to Char, Camus often travelled outside of Paris. He visited Janine and Michel Gallimard, who were in Switzerland in a hotel-sanatorium, as Michel, like Camus, suffered from tuberculosis. Then in January and February 1948 Camus went to Oran with Francine. He had told his friend Emmanuel Roblès that he would like to leave Paris, and Roblès found him a villa to buy. The villa was unfortunately sold to someone else, before Camus could reply to Roblès's letter.[156]

A chance meeting with Maria Casarès 18 June 1948 led to an affair which continued throughout Camus' life, although both would also have other lovers. They could not live together as Camus did not want to leave Francine because of the children. He respected Francine, but he was passionately in love with Maria. Francine found infidelity hard to understand.

René Char (1907–1988), born in southern France (often a subject of his poetry), was a strong man – a rugby player. He fought in the Resistance under the name Captaine Alexandre and was wounded. He had been aligned to the Surrealist movement before the war, but his later work was more devoted to ethical issues and to a questioning of the role of the poet. He published 20 volumes of poetry and is often considered the finest 20th-century French poet. Camus was in agreement with Char's political and philosophical opinions and discussed *The Rebel* as he was writing it with Char. Char was a model for the character of Rateau, the friend of the artist in Camus's story 'Jonas'. He corresponded with Camus regularly, from 1946–1959.

However the relationship between Maria and Albert was common knowledge, and he often came home early in the morning. His friends were aware that he could only really be happy with Maria, but that he also needed Francine in her role as mother and wife. The tension would continue for the rest of Camus' life. In 1949 he commented in his journals: *Once the slightest portion of the heart is subjected to duty, true love is impossible.* Francine represented duty. Another comment: *People insist on confusing marriage and love on the one hand, and love and happiness on the other. But they have nothing in common. That is why, the absence of love being more frequent than love, there are happy marriages.*[157]

In 1948 Camus completed another play, *L'Etat de Siège* (*State of Siege*), which was to be produced by Jean-Louis Barrault. *State of Siege* tells of an epidemic and of a community's reaction to it, but otherwise the plot bears no similarity to *The Plague*. A character named 'The Plague' is a political tyrant, who rules Cádiz, in Spain. A student, Diego, who rallies the people of the city against the tyrant, dies but the city is saved. From the beginning of the collaboration between Camus and Barrault, there were

Jean-Louis Barrault (1910–1994) was an actor, director and theatre manager. He acted in Marcel Carné's *The Children of Paradise* (1944), a film which also including Maria Casarès. His company, Compagnie Renaud-Barrault, founded with his wife Madeleine Renaud (1900–1994), also a famous actress, produced some of the most famous plays of the 20th century, as well as classical 17th century French theatre.

problems of interpretation. For Camus the plague was an absolute evil, whereas Barrault thought of the epidemic as a purifying disease.[158] *State of Siege* opened on the 27th of October 1948, with a stellar cast: Maria Casarès, Jean-Louis Barrault, Madeleine Renaud, the mime Marcel Marceau (1923–2007), among others. The famous composer Arthur

Honegger (1892–1955) wrote the music. Critics panned the production; as Camus noted in his preface to the collected plays: *When* State of Siege *first opened in Paris, there was no dissenting voice among the critics. Truly, few plays have ever enjoyed such a unanimous slashing.* Camus felt, however, that it was misjudged, as it was an allegorical drama. He even said that it was, *of all my writings, the one that most resembles me,* without explaining what that meant.[159] While working on his next play, he wrote to Francine: *I have lost all confidence in myself.*[160] Camus later felt that the play should have been staged in an open-air theatre, and would have liked to revive it.

State of Siege was attacked by Gabriel Marcel (1889–1973), a Christian existentialist philosopher and dramatist, who said that a play about tyranny should have been set in Eastern Europe, not in Spain. Camus replied in 'Why Spain?', in *Combat*, 25 November 1948: *Why this place, where for the first time Hitler, Mussolini, and Franco demonstrated to a world still asleep amid its comforts and its miserable morality what totalitarian methods were like?* The violence has not stopped; opponents of Franco are being sentenced to death. Marcel, he says, remains silent about Spain because *the murder of a human being elicits your outrage, apparently, only to the extent that the victim shares your ideas.*[161]

Although he knew so little about his own background, Camus felt close to Spain, where his maternal grandparents had come from. Fighting Franco's Spain was a cause he embraced since his first play, *Revolt in Asturia* in 1936. Now, in 1948, perhaps partly because of his love for Maria Casarès, he was increasingly active in the cause of republican Spain. He gave money to such organizations as a federation for Spanish refugees. He organized an appeal for a committee to support Spanish Republican émigrés, for which he obtained signatures, including those of René Char, Mauriac, Sartre.

In 1948 and '49, in spite of all he was writing, Camus found time to help organize the Groupes de Liaison Internationale, which was supported by anti-Stalinist left-wing intellectuals in the United States, including his friend Nicola Chiaromonte. The group's mission was to give assistance to victims of totalitarian regimes (in the Soviet Union, but also in Spain and Yugoslavia). They published a bulletin and held regular meetings. Eventually the movement was disbanded, without much concrete accomplishment, although the members of the group, many of whom had been revolutionaries, continued to be in contact. Among the group was Alfred Rosmer (1877–1964), who had been a trade union activist since 1914, a member of the Communist Party in the 1920s and then a Trotskyite, having realized that Stalin perverted the revolution. When Camus knew him, Rosmer, along with other former Communists, had quit writing for *L'Humanité*, the Communist daily paper. The Rosmers became friendly with Camus, Francine and the children. In 1953 Camus helped get Rosmer's *Moscou sous Lénine* (Moscow under Lenin) published; he wrote a preface in which he describes Rosmer as a man *who adhered with no reservations to the great experience of which he speaks in this book, who also recognized its perversion, but never used this failure to condemn the undertaking itself.* Rosmer refuses to *despair of the force of revolt and liberation that each of us feels.*[162]

Camus was attacked in Soviet magazines as a 'propagandist of decadent individualism', and also by right-wing commentators in France, one of whom (Roger Nimier) wrote of Camus's 'noble sentiments', and, unwittingly, said that France could not wage war 'with the lungs of Mr. Camus'.[163]

While Nimier did not know Camus was tubercular, and soon wrote a disclaimer, Camus never forgave him.

He had become a well-known celebrity and during July and August 1949, was sent by the French government on a cultural tour to South America. He visited Brazil, Uruguay, Argentina and Chile. The journal he kept of this trip is one of the most detailed of all his notebooks, giving a day-by-day report. From the beginning, on the ship, he mentions class distinctions, embarrassed by his first-class cabin after he sees the crowded fourth-class accommodation. He works conscientiously on the lectures he will give, makes observations about the sea, and ironic comments about the ship-board society. He is happy to be alone: *Either this stripped-down solitude or the storm of love - nothing else in the world interests me.* On this trip, however, he cannot find solitude, cannot avoid others, nor can he find love. He has a continual programme of lectures, seminars, and dinners, often with society women: *a lot of fancy hats!* In Brazil he had several occasions to observe such ceremonies as *macumba*, a mixture of Catholic and African beliefs, in which dancers become possessed since a god (Eshu or Ogun) enters them. Although he found material from observing ritual possessions to be used later for a short story ('La Pierre qui Pousse', 'The Growing Stone'), at the time he suffered from the heat and lack of air in the huts. He liked the courtesy of the Brazilian people and the mixture of racial types. He notes his own *reverse prejudice. I like blacks* à priori, *and I'm tempted to see in them qualities that they don't really have.* Recife is a *Florence of the tropics, between its coconut forests, its red mountains, its white beaches.* Often in his journal he complains of flu and fever, which cause him to be depressed. He writes on the 29th of July that he didn't really want to take the trip, and by the second of August notes: *what I realized clearly yesterday is that I want to die*, a surprising comment from the author of *The Myth of Sisyphus*, who philosophically rejected suicide. He could only write about the ocean trip, describing the sea poetically, two years later.[164]

When he returned to Paris on the 26th of August, he began to wonder if it was *not a question of something more than the grippe*. By October, it was clear that he did not have flu, but a major attack of tuberculosis. *End October '49. Relapse...* . *After so long a certainty of being cured, this recurrence ought to overwhelm me. It does in fact. But since I have been so uninterruptedly overwhelmed of late, it makes me want to laugh. At last I am free. Madness is also a liberation.*[165] He took large doses of streptomycin, needed bed rest, and even missed the dress rehearsal of his fourth play, *Les Justes* (*The Just Assassins*), which was first performed on the 15th of December 1949. It was again directed by Paul Oettly, with Maria Casarès in the leading role.

The Just Assassins is based on the history of the Russian revolutionaries of 1905, whose names are retained in the play. Camus' notebooks while he was working on the play contain detailed references to the sources he used, and continuing reflections on the moral problems posed by terrorism. As early as April 1946 he writes: *The only really serious moral problem is killing... . what must be discovered is whether I can kill this man in front of me, or allow him to be killed; and what must be understood is that I know nothing until I know if I can kill.*[166] The hero is Ivan Kaliayev, whose hatred of the oppression, represented here by the Grand Duke, has not destroyed his belief that men must conduct themselves with honour even when opposing tyranny. He will not bomb the royal carriage when he sees that the Grand Duke is accompanied by two children. After he succeeds in killing the Grand Duke in a later attempt, he refuses a pardon because he feels that his death will restore a moral balance: *If I did not die – it's then I'd be a murderer.*[167]

To the reader today this moral may seem to justify suicide bombers. As Jean Daniel wrote in 2006, in an age when children are bearing arms, such problems are new and complex. The denunciation of the massacre of innocents, however, is still obvious, 'everywhere and always', and 'in the terms that Camus expressed'.[168] When another revolutionary says *Provided justice is done–even if it's done by assassins – what does it matter?*, Ivan says this attitude constitutes *the threat of another despotism*, an implied criticism of the Communist position that the end can justify the means. Kaliayev wants to kill only one man. His lover, Dora Doulebov, wonders whether even that limited project can be justified. When Ivan says *When we kill, we're killing so as to build up a world in which there will be no more killing*, she replies, *And suppose it didn't work out like that?* After Ivan's execution, she adds: *It's easy, ever so much easier, to die of one's inner conflicts than to live with them.*[169] As in many of his works, Camus introduces complexity and undermines easy heroism. Meursault, Rieux, Caligula - none are exemplary heroes of revolt. Nor is Ivan. As Camus noted: *A life is paid for by a life. The reasoning is fallacious but worthy of respect?*[170] In the 1958 preface to the play he wrote: *action itself has limits. There is no good and just action but what recognizes those limits and, if it must go beyond them, at least accepts death.*[171] This is not a message for revolutionaries or suicide bombers.

As well as snippets from his readings and phrases to use in his works, Camus's notebooks by 1950 contain more personal references, which show his frequent uncertainty: *I lived*

*the whole of my youth with the idea of my innocence, that
is to say with no idea at all. Today ... .* He finds that in his
notebooks *landscapes disappear, little by little. The modern
cancer is eating me away too. Memory going more and more.*
He notes in February 1950, *Perhaps in April when I shall
have found a freedom again,* presumably a reference to some
freedom after the completion of *The Rebel.*[172]

The first volume of his 'Contemporary Essays', *Actuelles
I,* was published in 1950. Camus remained at odds with the
left-wing intellectuals who dominated the press in Paris.
Undoubtedly the need to define his own position against
partisan political programmes was a reason to publish this
collection of essays. It includes a number of editorials from
Combat, from those celebrating the liberation of Paris to the
more pessimistic editorials grouped as 'Two Years Later'. He
also reprints his replies to the criticism of Emmanuel d'Astier
de la Vigerie and Gabriel Marcel. He was increasingly disturbed at the compromises he had made in claiming that the
Soviet Union and the Western capitalists were equally to be
condemned. In March 1950 he wrote in his notebooks: *I feel
as if I am waking up after a ten-year sleep - still entangled
with the bandages of unhappiness and false moralities ... it is
only belatedly that we have the courage of what we know.*[173]

Because of illness, he took a year's sick leave from Gallimard, and went to Cabris, on the hills behind the French
Riviera, to write. He was happy to be away from Paris, as
he had more in common with René Char than with Parisian
intellectuals. Camus did not have extravagant tastes, being
content with an old car, travelling in second-class compart-
ments on the train. He was often scandalized by the luxurious
life of the rich. He made other friends in the south of France,
and was now in a position to help them financially; among

these was Urbain Polge, a pharmacist, who also had a love of literature.

He spent some time in Le Panelier (where he had stayed during the war) and in nearby Chambon-sur-Lignon. Sometimes he was joined by his wife and children, sometimes by the three Faure women, Francine's mother and two sisters, to whom she was profoundly attached. He escaped in August 1950 to spend a month with Maria Casarès in a small village in the Vosges mountains. He was by then a property owner, having bought an apartment in Paris. There he was again surrounded by Francine's family, from whom he often fled. He preferred to work in a hotel room: *I have never been able to succumb to what is called home life (so often the very opposite of an inner life); 'bourgeois' happiness bores and terrifies me.*[174]

During February 1951 he was living alone in the South of France, working feverishly on *The Rebel*. Although he writes to Francine that he wonders if he has really succeeded in doing what he set out to do,[175] by the seventh of March 1951 he notes that the first version of *The Rebel* is done. It was a project that had taken years and when it was finished, he hoped it would bring freedom. He could not have anticipated that its publication would result in so much conflict.

Albert Camus and Jean Grenier photographed in 1952.

7
1951–56: The Rebel and The Fall

Published in October 1951, *The Rebel* examines the concepts 'Rebellion' and 'Revolution'. Although France has had four revolutions since 1789 without establishing a free, democratic society equal to that in Scandinavia, French intellectuals have idealized 'Revolution'. Many intellectuals, as Camus knew, overlooked the police state and concentration camps of the Soviet Union to preserve the myth of 'Revolution'.

His essay is a plea for tolerance and limits. He analyses political and philosophical movements to show how the search for justice usually sacrifices men for some long-range ideal. He does not accept any eschatological system: neither Communism, which justifies oppression in the name of a classless society to be established in the future, nor Christianity, in which men suffer in this world to be happy in the next. There will be no 'pie in the sky by and by'. 'Revolution' leads to authoritarian dictatorship. 'Rebellion', in contrast, is based on a belief in a common human dignity; it is limited and does not aspire to change the world, for it recognizes that the world is not entirely evil and that men are not naturally virtuous.

In a discussion of 'Rebellion and Art' he analyses the rise

of the novel in the 18th and 19th centuries during a time of political upheaval. The novel translates to an aesthetic plane the same desire to remake the world that motivates revolutions: *What, in fact, is a novel but a universe in which action is endowed with form, where final words are pronounced, where people possess one another completely ... The world of the novel is only a rectification of the world we live in.* Art, however, cannot change the real world. Like the limited rebellion Camus advocates, art teaches man that he is human and not divine.[176]

In the concluding chapters, Camus writes that *every thought, every action that goes beyond a certain point negates itself,* but that rebellion *brings to light the measure and the limit which are the very principle* of human nature. *At this meridian of thought, the rebel thus rejects divinity in order to share in the struggles and destiny of all men. We shall choose Ithaca, the faithful land, frugal and audacious thought, lucid action, and the generosity of the man who understands.* It is understandable that some would find Camus' programme a bit vague. As Camus knew, he was an artist, not a philosopher or a political activist. He had, however, correctly defined the need to condemn ideologies that allow the end to justify the means.[177]

In a letter to Francine in November 1951, Camus wrote: *since the book came out, I have been in an awful state, which has become worse the last few days. I'm not sure I can any longer put up with this job and its lonely trials.*[178] In December 1951 he noted: *I'm waiting patiently for the slow catastrophe to come,* and added that he felt too alone.[179] Since the disappearance of *Combat,* he never felt supported by the warmth of other people. The catastrophe was much more than he had anticipated.

The Rebel was first attacked by André Breton (1896–1966), a poet and the theorist of the Surrealist movement, who scoffed at the idea that rebellion could include a concept of 'measure' and 'limitation'. There was, however, a sort of reconciliation between Camus and Breton at a meeting to protest treatment of labour leaders in Spain, to which Camus had asked that Breton be invited.

Much more serious was the attack from the political Left. Jean Grenier, who read the manuscript of *The Rebel*, had warned Camus that it would be seen as reactionary and that he would have many enemies.[180] Grenier was correct. Most of the intellectuals in France in the 1950s were at least sympathetic to the Soviet Union. When Czeslaw Milosz (1911- 2004), a Polish poet and later Nobel Prize winner, left Stalinist Poland in 1951, Camus was, he said, one of the few to help him. 'Others considered him something of a leper or a sinner against the "future"'.[181] Camus also supported the Mexican writer Octavio Paz (1914–1998), who had been in Spain during the Spanish civil war, and was pro-Republican. The Left marginalized Paz after he became disillusioned with Communism in the 1950s.

There were favourable reviews from the non-Communist Left, 60,800 copies sold in the first four months. Then came a savage review in Sartre's *Les Temps modernes* in May 1952. Written not by Sartre but by a young colleague, Francis Jeanson, the title, 'Albert Camus ou l'âme révoltée' (Albert Camus or the rebel soul), plays on Camus's title, suggesting that he is interested not in man (*l'homme*) but in the soul (*l'âme*), not in political realities but in some vague idealism. Already, Jeanson writes, *The Plague* advocated a 'Red Cross ethics'. Jeanson praises Camus' style, only to mock the content of the essay, especially the attack on Marx.

Camus was given the chance to respond. The August issue of *Les Temps modernes* included Camus' response (17 pages), Sartre's reply to Camus (20 pages) and Jeanson's reply (30 pages). Camus was often sarcastic; he was *tired of being lectured to by censors who had never pointed anything but their armchairs in the direction of history*.[182] Sartre descends to the personal, accusing Camus of using his humble origins to pretend to defend the poor: 'It is possible that you were poor, but you no longer are; you are bourgeois like Jeanson and me.'[183] The 'it is possible' is, of course, Sartre's refusal to acknowledge what he knew about Camus's origins. Sartre continues by mocking Camus's knowledge of philosophy. Beyond the *ad hominem* attacks, the dispute is over the contrasting attitudes to Communism. Although Sartre was never a member of the Party, the Soviet Union was, for him, the image of socialism. Sartre felt that one must support the Russians, not the Americans.

Sartre's *Les Temps modernes* was founded in 1945, and published by Gallimard in its first years, and again from 1985 on. It has published works by many famous authors from various countries. Its editorial board included Simone de Beauvoir and Merleau-Ponty, as well as Francis Jeanson (1922–2009), who was in 1952 one of the younger members of the board. He became an active supporter of the National Liberation Front in the war in Algeria. Later he wrote biographical studies of both Sartre and de Beauvoir.

Sartre moved on from the controversy. Camus, however, was shattered. Many, even among the editors at Gallimard, thought Sartre had won the argument and would not talk to Camus about it. He could seem sanctimonious, self-consciously aware of his honour. He was vulnerable to criticism, which he could not easily brush off. In September he wrote to his wife: *I'm paying dearly for this unhappy book. Today I have doubts about it - and about myself.*[184] He wrote a 20-page defence of *The Rebel*, which was never published. He had always felt out of place among the French intelligentsia, as he came from a poor social background – a provincial town and a university rather than one of the *grandes écoles* (the elite centres for educating top philosophers, historians and political leaders). He was sometimes considered 'vulgar' because of his lowly origins.[185] In *The First Man* Camus notes: *What they did not like in him was the Algerian*.[186]

He could not write anything new, but did put together a second collection of essays, *Actuelles II* ('Contemporary Articles, Volume 2'), many of them concerning the polemics about *The Rebel*. 'The Artist and his Time' is a compilation of questions put together from various interviews, questions that gave him the opportunity to defend himself from attacks and to explain his position. He finds *opportunities for action in the relative. Trade-unionism is today the first and the most fruitful among them*. To an interviewer who wants to know if he is quixotic or idealistic, he replies: *I am arguing in favor of a true realism against a mythology that is both illogical and deadly, and against romantic nihilism whether it be bourgeois or allegedly revolutionary. I cannot keep from being drawn toward everyday life, toward those, whoever they may be, who are humiliated and debased*. He adds that we must *reject the bitterness*, but his own bitterness and defensiveness are often apparent.[187] He refused to sign a letter prepared by Sartre's magazine in favour of a sailor who protested the war in Indochina: *it would compromise the value of liberty, among other values, to defend them in cooperation with* Les Temps modernes.[188] In spite of the emotional turmoil caused by *The Rebel*, he said in 1954 that it was his most important book.[189] He had received many letters of support, including some from Eastern Europe, which helped moderate his despair at the attacks by French intellectuals.

Towards the end of 1952 he noted that he no longer believed in his star, but after the publication of *Actuelles II* in October 1953 he wrote that the 'stock-taking' was now finished, and he could create again.[190] Creation, however, came slowly. He edited *Été* (*Summer*), a collection of his lyrical essays written at various times, for the most part about Algeria. In 'Return to Tipasa' he describes a visit to the Roman ruins 20 years after the visit recounted in *Nuptials*. Memories of Tipasa have saved him from despair, for life in Europe has been unsatisfying: *In the clamor we live in, love is impossible and justice not enough.*[191] The essay was written after a visit to Algeria in November 1951, to be with his mother, who was hospitalized for surgery. She was one of the few people for whom Camus could feel a deep love that was not *impossible*. The only other essay for *Summer* written in 1953 after *The Rebel* was published is 'The Sea Close By', poetically describing his trip to South America in 1948.

Camus continued to write and speak about abuse especially in Soviet-controlled Eastern Europe and in Franco's Spain. He also wrote to the Argentine ambassador to protest the arrest by the Peron government of his friend Victoria Ocampo (1890–1979), the editor of *Sur*, a major literary magazine in Argentine, whom he had visited in 1948. He joined in a rally on the 30th of June 1953, protesting against the brutal suppression of workers in East Germany by the Soviet forces.

In the midst of Camus's anguish and feeling of being blocked from new creative writing, personal problems arose. In the autumn of 1953 Francine suffered from depression. As she needed constant attention, Camus took her to Oran, to be with her family. She was then moved to a clinic on the outskirts of Paris, where she jumped out a window and fractured her pelvis. Her sister Christiane thought Francine was trying to escape from the clinic; Camus thought it was a suicide attempt. Although there had been mental illnesses in Francine's family, the Faures blamed her depression on Camus, who felt responsible and thought that when she recovered she should seek a legal separation. For a time one of the twins, Jean, was cared for by his friends, the Polges, in southern France, and the other, Catherine, was with her aunt in Oran. Towards the end of 1954 Francine was given electric shock treatment.[192]

The Italian Cultural Association invited Camus in 1954 to give lectures. He comments in his notebook: *Lecture. In the evening I take the train to Rome, exasperated by the stupid social rituals that follow lectures. Can't stand more than half an hour of such nonsense.* Later, when he was able to plan his own travel, among the ruins in Paestum, he could, as he did in Tipasa, relax deeply. Italy made him regret the *stupid, dark years I've spent in Paris.*[193] While he was in Italy he learned that Simone de Beauvoir was awarded the Prix Goncourt in 1954 for her novel *The Mandarins*. Although she said that the novel was not a *roman à clé* (based on real people), it closely follows certain events in the lives of Camus, Sartre and de Beauvoir. Perron (Camus) has a wife who is ill and whom he does not love. He has a mistress who is an actress. He is praised by the conservative press. At times de Beauvoir attributes some of Sartre's habits, such as drug-taking, to Camus. The caricature of Perron is often nasty. He is said to so admire Dubreuilh (Sartre) that he apes him. Worse, Perron is said to protect someone who collaborated with the Nazis and had given information to the Gestapo. Camus wrote in his notebook (12 December 1954) that, except for making him editor of a Resistance paper, everything was false (although of course the comments about his wife and mistress were mostly accurate). Ironically, he adds: *even better, the dubious things that Sartre did are generously attributed to me.* He calls the whole prize circus in France *a farce.*[194]

During the years following the controversy about *The Rebel*, Camus needed to defend his positions and his work. In 1954 he had a typed copy prepared of the first seven of his notebooks, for the years 1935–1951, with a view to later publication. He removed passages that he felt were too personal. (The notebooks were not in fact published until after his death.)[195] In 1958 he wrote a preface to the republication of his early *The Wrong Side and the Right Side*, in which he finds the source of his work *in the world of poverty and sunlight I lived in for so long*,[196] a rebuttal of Sartre's claim that Camus was 'bourgeois'. In the 1958 preface to the American edition of his plays, Camus is defensive about their critical reception. *Caligula* is not meant to be shocking, but only shows *an immoderate devotion to truth*. Of *State of Siege* he writes *I am still convinced that my attempt deserves attention* and adds a footnote that the play has been performed in Yugoslavia. He believes theatre should *involve human fate in all its simplicity and grandeur* and not rely on *ingenious plot-devices* or *spicy situations.*[197]

He turned increasingly towards the theatre. In 1953 he became director of the second season of the Angers theatre festival, where, in the courtyard of a 13th-century castle, plays were presented, including two of his adaptations: *Les Esprits* (The Spirits), a 16th-century drama by Pierre de Larivey (1541–1619), which Camus had begun working on around 1940; and *Dévotion à la Croix* (Devotion to the Cross), by Pedro Calderon (1600–1681), which he translated from Spanish with considerable assistance from Maria Casarès, as his Spanish was limited. Maria also appeared in both productions, as did Paul Oettly (who had directed *Caligula*). At this time Camus met Robert Cérésol, the deputy director of the Mathurins theatre in Paris, who became a good friend. Camus also began working on an adaptation of Dostoyevsky's *The Possessed*, a project that would take him six years.

Earlier, even before *The Rebel* was published, Camus made a list of stories to write, jotting down some sentences and ideas to use. Slowly he began writing creatively again. After a visit to southern Algeria, an area he did not know, he describes in his notebook the landscape that would be the setting for three of the stories in *Exile and the Kingdom*. He also started making notes towards what would become *The First Man*. 'La Femme adultère' ('The Adulterous Wife'), the first story in *Exile and the Kingdom,* was completed by 1954, and published separately in an illustrated edition. He was, however, uncertain about his 'star'. In a letter to René Char, of 7 August 1954, he said that he no longer knew how to write.[198]

His notebooks often still contain echoes of the controversy with Sartre. He lists what the 'collaborationist' Left approves, or at least accepts silently: the physical destruction of the Russian peasant class, anti-Semitism, political executions behind the Iron Curtain. He finds fault with 'existentialism': *According to our existentialists, every man is responsible for what he is. This explains the complete disappearance of compassion in their universe of aggressive old men.* He needed to define his political and philosophical positions. On the fall of Dien Bien Phu (7 May 1954)which marked the end of the French occupation of Vietnam (then still called French Indochina), he blames both the Right and the Left for the massacre of the French forces. An entry of 1 November 1954 defines his religious belief: *I don't believe in God and I am not an atheist*. For Camus an atheist is satisfied with the world without God, but the anguish of an unknowable world in which men die meant he could never have such satisfaction.[199]

In October 1954 Camus visited Holland, under the auspices of the French government. A new story was taking shape, to be set in Amsterdam, which he described in his notebooks. commenting on the continual rain, the greyness: *Holland, sweet Holland, where you learn the patience to die.*[200] He only stayed in Amsterdam for four days, but they included some hours at the Mexico-City bar, a meeting place for sailors and prostitutes. It became the setting for *La Chute* (*The Fall*), which grew from a story to a full-length work. When I visited the Mexico-City bar in 1958, the proprietor, to whom Camus had sent a copy of his book, admired the true-to-life description of the bar and remembered the author sitting in the corner writing. Camus enjoyed the company of the fringe elements of society, including prostitutes.[201]

During February 1955 Camus visited Algeria, where revolt against the French forces had already begun. From the 26th of April to the 11th of May, under official government sponsorship, he took a long postponed trip to Greece, for him the source of Mediterranean culture and its notion of 'measure', opposed to the extremes of northern Europe. In Greece, unlike during former sponsored tours, he was happy and did not complain about needing to give lectures. Seeing an archaeologist at work, he comments: *I envy him a little and blame myself bitterly for the time lost these last few years.* Watching archaeologists at a dig, he writes: *I have never been happy and satisfied except in a job, work accomplished with other men that I can love. I don't have a job, but only a vocation. And my work is solitary.*[202]

Jacques Servan-Schreiber, editor of the French news magazine *L'Express*, wanted to add Camus to his roster of writers. Camus' friend, Jean Daniel, one of the editors, agreed to approach him. A letter was sent during his trip to Greece. He replied with an article on the excavation of some Greek ruins, which Servan-Schreiber thought of limited interest to his readership. Daniel said, if you want Camus, publish it. After its publication Camus agreed to write for *L'Express*, primarily because the magazine was in favour of Pierre Mendès France (1907–1982), leader of the centrist Radical party. Mendès France, Camus believed, was the only political figure to *respect equally the rights of the Arabs and those of the French*.[203] Camus wrote 35 articles for *L'Express*, over a period of more than nine months, often on Algeria. He was always a serious journalist, commenting ironically on the story of Princess Margaret and Townsend that it *will have permitted us … to be distracted from the trivialities of life*.[204] Daniel realized that Camus was not at ease with the magazine and disliked its advertising techniques, but that he was happy to be a journalist once again. After Guy Mollet (1905–1975), the Socialist leader, became the head of the government rather than Mendès France, Camus sent his final article (on Mozart) to the paper on 2 February 1956.[205] He quit partly because *L'Express* was willing to consider the possibility of independence for Algeria, which he was not.

By February 1956 Camus had finished *The Fall*. Unusually for him, it is not a work that slowly matured over several years, with many notations in his notebooks, nor is it included in his notebooks of 1952 in the list of stories to be written. *The Fall* is unlike Camus's earlier writing, and unlike most of the stories that would make up *Exile and the Kingdom*. If, however, the story came to him more quickly, *The Fall* also required much rewriting. It went through seven revisions.[206] The first clear indications of what was on his mind are from 20 and 21 September 1954, just before his short visit to Holland: *God is not necessary to create guilt or punishment. Human beings are sufficient. How can anyone preach justice when he can't make it control his own life?*[207]

The Fall is a monologue, in which Jean-Baptiste Clamence (John the Baptist, who proclaims [*clamer*] clemency) speaks to an unidentified listener in the Mexico City bar. Clamence was a successful Parisian attorney who gave up his career to live in the Amsterdam underworld, where he defends thieves and procurers. He confesses the ways in which he is guilty, only to turn the tables at the end to make others guilty as well. He sees his role as that of a *judge penitent*, whose penitence gives him the right to be a judge.

One night, going home across the Pont des Arts in Paris (the Bridge of Arts, a significant location for a story referring indirectly to Camus himself), he felt that the world was laughing at him; his facade of happiness, innocence and self-contentment crumbled. Later he confesses that there was an earlier incident on a bridge, when he saw a young girl who jumped into the water, then cried for help. He made no effort to rescue her. Realizing that he was cowardly, he tries to avoid facing his conscience, first by acting the fool, next by orgies of drunkenness and sexual debauchery. He then moves to Amsterdam, a city he hates for its dampness, but which he chooses as a means of self-mortification, and because its circular canals resemble the circles of Hell in Dante's *Inferno*. As he re-examines his earlier life, he decides that every act he thought virtuous reveals a profound egotism. The sexual relationships he thought were satisfying now seem a way of dominating others. His aid to victims of injustice appears as a means of self-aggrandizement. He is guilty, but so is every-one. Even Christ was guilty because his life was saved by the massacre of the Innocents.

Since there is no universally accepted judge, Clamence himself becomes the *judge penitent*. As Jean-Baptiste he wishes to be the prophet of a new religion of guilt and slavery: *on the bridges of Paris I too learned that I was afraid of freedom. So hurrah for the master, whoever he may be, to take the place of heaven's law*.[208] Clamence's system shares features of Marxism as Camus described it in *The Rebel*. After the 'Revolution' comes *the affirmation of general culpa-bility. Every man is a criminal who is unaware of being so*.[209] In his notebook, in December 1954, he linked judge-penitents to the existentialists: *When they accuse themselves you can be sure that it's always in order to heap insults on others*.[210] Because the novel was often misinterpreted, Camus added an epigraph to the English-language translation of *The Fall*, to underline the satiric intent. Clamence is *a portrait but not of an individual; it is the aggregate of the vices of our whole generation*.

Many saw Clamence as a portrait of one individual, Camus himself. Clamence's life in Paris may seem initially a portrait of Camus's own. He is successful, has many friends, likes to dance, loves sports and the theatre and is attractive to women. Just as Clamence was a respected lawyer, Camus was a journalist and public figure defended humanitarian causes. Like Clamence, Camus loved heights and had a claustropho-bic fear of enclosed places, which he attributed to sclerosis of his lungs. More intimately, the refusal to help a young woman jumping from a bridge is an indirect reference to Francine's suicide attempts, as she herself realized.[211] Camus replied to a letter from an unnamed correspondent, who thought that her friend was the source of Clamence, and that Camus knew something about this man's failure to help prevent a suicide. Of course not, he says: *I swear on my honour that the details in* The Fall *only concern me... . As for the main incident . . let me quote a letter I just received from one of my friends: 'Each of us, without exception, has in his life a young girl that he did not help.'*[212]

After the publication of *The Rebel*, Camus' life had changed; he was under attack. He lost his self-confidence. Jeanson accused him of being self-righteous and politically ineffective: 'You aren't on the right, Camus, you're in the air'. Clamence refers ironically to Jeanson's criticism: *I was not on the floor of the courtroom but somewhere in the flies like those gods that are brought down by machinery from time to time to transfigure the action.*[213] Clamence becomes a portrait of Camus as Sartre and Jeanson saw him. If it contains considerable self-criticism, the novel also is strongly critical of the left-wing intellectuals who attacked Camus. The bitterness lying beneath the satire shows the extent to which Camus had changed since the hopes he expressed in his *Combat* editorials after the war: *we have lost track of the light, the mornings, the holy innocence of those who forgive themselves.*[214] Although Camus still felt, as he wrote in a letter to René Char, that *the more I produce the less I am sure*,[215], *The Fall* is the most accomplished of his writing since *The Stranger*. Published in May 1956, it received mixed reactions, but has later been judged a masterpiece.

By 1956 Camus no longer lived with Francine; he rented a small apartment where he could work. However, he continued, however, to spend time each summer with the children. Even if he was not a good husband, he tried to be a good father. He finished an adaptation of William Faulkner's novel

Requiem for a Nun for the theatre, which he was to direct in Paris. Due to Francine's depression he did not want his name associated publicly with Maria Casarès. He began to look for actors, especially the female lead, and often went to plays to spot possible talent. In May he found Catherine Sellers, who would be the next love of his life, a love affair that started in September. Olivier Todd describes the complications of Camus's relationship to the women he loved: 'Maria and Catherine accept their competition or their complementary roles and are aware of Albert's attachment to Francine and the obligations this entails. Maria puts up with Camus's occasional straying, his adventures, with more tolerance than Catherine.'[216] In a rare reference to any of his lovers, Camus describes Catherine's relationship to her father in his notebook: *Died deported to Birkenau. Typhus. Cremated in an oven; 'I always remember that he had some gold in his teeth.' … C. loved him. Her life began when she landed here when she was 16.*[217]

Catherine Sellers (1928-), whose career had started shortly before she began working with Camus, has since become a major actress on stage and in films. She was born of North African Jewish parents, and lived during the war in Algeria. Her father, a doctor, was deported and killed in Birkenau. She studied literature and wrote a thesis on Elizabethan theatre. Well educated and articulate, she helped Camus with his theatre projects.

Camus spent part of the summer of 1956 in the South of France where his mother visited him. Then he returned to Paris for the rehearsals of *Requiem for a Nun*. He was an energetic director, stressing the importance of body movements, working the actors for many hours. By the time of the opening night, the 22nd of September 1956, the cast had gone through 70 rehearsals. The play was a great success financially as well as with the critics.

A portrait of Albert Camus.

8

1954–1958: Exile and the Kingdom, The Nobel Prize and Algeria once more

The political situation in Algeria, with the eruption of violence, badly affected Camus. He belonged to the community of those of European origin who had lived in Algeria, many for nearly a century. His community was not the rich *colons* (those who made their wealth from exploiting the resources and the workers of Algeria), but the working class. From his first investigations as a journalist in Algiers, Camus had been aware of how the native population in Algeria was treated poorly by the French administration. He had advocated policies that would lead towards the assimilation of the Muslim population into the political society, defending the Blum-Violette bill in 1937 that proposed the gradual extension of the vote to those of non-European origin. The bill was not enacted into law. By the 1930s there were about 900,000 settlers of European origin and 6,000,000 Arabs and Berbers. Between 1865 and 1962, however, only 7,000 Muslims in Algeria became French citizens. Camus quit the Communist Party in large part because of its refusal to address the issue of Muslim rights. When he visited Algeria during the Sétif riots in 1945, he was already aware that the time for assimilation was passing.

While living in France, Camus often tried to help North Africans in trouble with the French government. In November 1951 he prepared an affidavit for the defence of Muslim nationalists belonging to Messali Hadj's party who were on trial for subversive activities.[218] In early 1954 seven Tunisians were condemned to death for having killed three policemen. Camus wrote to the French president: *A few days later I had my reply in the newspapers. Three of the condemned had been executed.* Two weeks after the execution, *a director of the president's cabinet informed me that my letter had 'received the attention' of the president... . Bureaucracy out of touch.*[219] When on 14 July 1953 Hadj's supporters clashed with the police in Paris, who opened fire and killed seven Muslims, Camus wrote to *Le Monde*, a major French newspaper, to protest the charges filed against the North Africans, and the action of the police.[220]

After the armed revolt of the Muslim population in Algeria began on the first of November 1954, with attacks by the FLN (National Liberation Front) on army camps and police stations, Camus rejected the violence. He was torn between sympathy for the demands of the native population and a desire to keep open the possibility for a continued union of Algeria with France. He felt Algerian; Algeria was his home, not France. According to Jean Daniel, as early as 1947, Camus knew that *Algérie française* (French Algeria, the continuation of Algeria as a part of a greater France, under conditions similar to those applied since colonization in 1830) was finished.[221] French politicians, however, including Mendès France, whom Camus supported, still said that

Algeria was an integral part of the French Republic. Camus hoped to find a solution in which the two communities could live together, in which the rights of the Muslim and the French populations would be equal. Those of French origin living in Algeria, known as the *pieds noirs* (literally 'black feet', a name whose origin has never been explained), were for Camus different from metropolitan French. He describes 'Algerians' (by which he means here the French Algerians, the *pieds noirs*): *Their life is in the depth and warmth of friendship, of the family. The body is central... . Proud of their virility, of their capacity to eat and drink, of their force and their courage. Vulnerable.*[222]

He recommended that the Algerian legislature be dissolved and a new, more representative election be held. This legislature could handle internal problems and the French legislature, with Algerian representatives, could treat the problems of a French-Algerian federation. In a 'Letter to an Algerian militant', 1955, addressed to Aziz Kessous (1903–1965), an Algerian socialist, Camus wrote: *we are condemned to live together*. He could not accept the possibility of the French Algerian population being forced to leave, their only home was Algeria, and they were not, *all bloodthirsty rich men*.[223] This theme recurs frequently in Camus' essays. French Algerians were often poor, and sympathetic to the Muslim population; three-quarters of the French Algerians, like those in his own family, never exploited anyone. The standard of living of the French Algerians was at least 20% less than that of French in France.[224] Camus's family in Algeria in the 1950s included his mother and uncle, his brother and his children; they should not be confused with the rich colonials.

During August 1955, violence escalated, with the massacre of 71 Europeans and 52 Muslims. In retaliation 1,273 rebels were killed. By 1955, there were 2,000,000 French soldiers in Algeria, mostly young men doing their compulsory military service. To keep in touch Camus asked for news from Charles Poncet, a friend from his youth, a fellow traveller in the 1930s, now a supporter of equal rights for the Muslim population. Camus, who was in contact with his mother by phone, told Jean Grenier that his mother was terrified because in Belcourt an Arab shopkeeper had been knifed. When she came to Paris, however, she found the streets too calm, with too few people to look at: 'What do you expect, there aren't any Arabs' she told her son. She did not want to live in France, and he understood that.[225] Camus copied the comment in his notebook, to use for *The First Man*.[226] Her home, and his too, was in Algeria.

In January 1956 he agreed to speak in Algiers on behalf of a group hoping to find a way of bringing the two communities together. On his arrival he met with Charles Poncet, who had urged him to come, and with Yves Dechezelles (1912–2006), a college classmate, member of the League of Human Rights and the lawyer for Messali Hadj. He noted on 18 January: *The anguish I felt in Paris about Algeria has left me. Here at least we are in the fight, hard for us, with public opinion against us. But it's in fighting that I have always found peace. An intellectual by profession ... lives like a coward. He compensates for his impotence by verbal exaggeration... . Yes, I woke up happy for the first time in months. I have found my star again.*[227]

A meeting to appeal for a civil truce was arranged, which Emmanuel Roblès was to chair, to include French Algerians and Muslims (who were often secretly members of the FLN). The extreme right-wing French, who wanted to retain 'French Algeria' made plans to sabotage the meeting. Camus felt that his own life might be threatened and, after first rejecting the need for protection, arranged for bodyguards. The meeting took place on the 22nd of January 1956. Camus had agreed to speak only if representatives of the Muslim population included Ferhat Abbas. Abbas came in late. 'He arrived while Camus was speaking. Interrupted by unusual applause, Camus turned, saw Abbas, and greeted him with an embrace while the audience cheered wildly, seized with emotion and a mad hope: would everything still be possible?' During Camus' speech, however, there were also cries of protest from the audience outside, against Camus, Mendès France, and even Jews. The extremists threw rocks at the windows, Camus read his text rapidly and the meeting was quickly adjourned. Camus 'feared that his attempt to humanize the conflict and to bring the communities together would degenerate into a bloody confrontation between them.'[228]

By the time of the meeting, the situation was worsening. The best Camus could hope was that both the Arab movement and the French authorities would *declare simultaneously that for the duration of the fighting the civilian population will on every occasion be respected and protected.*[229] Camus' appeal came to nothing. Guy Mollet, the prime minister, ignored it; the FLN said they were open to discussion, but in vague terms. When Mollet came to Algiers on the sixth of February, he was pelted with tomatoes by the *pieds noirs*, who feared the government would give too much to the Muslims; Mollet gave in to the *pieds noirs* demands. Camus was disillusioned. The settlers had chosen. There were now only two sides. Censorship was soon established in Algeria. As violence escalated, the FLN attacked not only the French army and the French Algerian civilian population, but even those Muslims who did not agree with them. In 1956 the FLN massacred 374 Algerians suspected of sympathy with Messali Hadj.

Jean de Maisonseul (1912–1999), an artist and a town planner, a friend of Camus from his youth, and a member of the committee for the civil truce appeal, was arrested 26 May 1956, framed on a charge of treason. Camus wrote two protest letters to newspapers. Eventually Maisonseul's case was moved to Paris where it was not settled until after de Gaulle came to power in 1958. In 1957 Camus met with Germaine Tillion (1907- 2008), a noted ethnographer, who had worked in Algeria and sought equal rights for the Muslim population. She described to him her encounter with several FLN militants, whom she told to stop their violence, treating them like naughty school boys. She also showed Camus the essays that 30 Arab boys of 11 or 12 had written on the subject 'What would you do if you were invisible?' *They all would take up arms and kill either the French or the paras* (the crack military units who often tortured rebels) *or the leaders of the government.* Camus noted: *I despair of the future.*[230]

His fiction was influenced by the political situation in Algeria and often reflects his own feelings in relation to his native land. In *Exile and the Kingdom*, four of the six stories are set in Algeria, and express the often tense relationship of French Algerians to the Muslim population (which Camus, as was common at the time, almost always refers to as *Arabs*). The stories are written in varying registers and styles, *from an interior monologue to a realistic story*, but all treat of the theme of exile. Like Camus himself, the characters feel exiled from the world they seek; they are aware of their ageing bodies and have reached a point of crisis. The kingdom *coincides with a certain free, naked life that we must find again, to be reborn.*[231].

In 'La Femme Adultère' ('The Adulterous Wife'), when

a French woman goes with her husband on a sales tour in the Algerian desert, she becomes aware of the vast contrast between her life – with its bourgeois routine, its lack of physical vitality and its dependence on material possessions – and the life of the nomadic tribes she sees, who, she feels, live in physical harmony with the world around them. Late at night she goes from her hotel room to a terrace overlooking the desert, to commit a symbolic act of adultery with a purer world. Rather like Meursault, at the end of *The Stranger*, she opens herself to the *gentle indifference of the world*. It is, however, a temporary deliverance, as she must return to her husband, and to the more restricted world of the French Algerians.

'Le Renégat' ('The Renegade, or a Confused Mind') is a powerful poetic monologue, filled with strong masochistic eroticism, spoken by a French Catholic priest who has tried to convert a fierce, isolated tribe in the Algerian desert, but who, after he is tortured and humiliated, converts to their religion of hatred. Jean Grenier told Camus he didn't understand the story; Camus explained that it was a parable of a modern acceptance of totalitarianism by left-wing intellectuals impatient with humanist traditions.[232] The story could also be seen as a portrait of a Christian whose absolute religious truth is conquered by another truth, which might be considered Marxist.

'Les Muets' ('The Voiceless') is a simpler, more realistic story of workers in a cooperage in Algiers, who quarrel with the boss. He cannot meet their demands for higher wages and they cannot sympathize with him when his child becomes critically ill. Both employer and employees are imprisoned in a world of exile and death.

Daru, the schoolmaster in a small village on the Algerian

plateau in 'L'Hôte' ('The Guest'), is asked to deliver an Arab prisoner who had killed another Arab in a brawl to the police. Instead he sets the prisoner free, telling him to choose between going to the town to be judged or escaping to the hills where nomadic tribes will give him protection. The Arab takes the road towards judgment. Returning to the school, Daru finds a message on the blackboard: *You handed over our brother. You will pay for this.* Neither the Europeans nor the Arabs understand him. *In this vast landscape he had loved so much, he was alone.*[233] Like Camus, Daru can belong wholly to neither community, but he rejects any cooperation with violence. In his notebooks, in 1955, after the Algerian war had started, Camus suggests another possible ending, an ambiguity that he did not use in the finished story: *'The Guest'. The prisoner takes the road to the prison, but Daru deceived him, and showed him the road to liberty.*[234] Camus was uncertain about the role he could play in the increasing trouble in Algeria. The French title of this story could mean either 'the guest' or 'the host'. Who is the host here, Daru who gives the Arab food and shelter, or the Arab, whose country has been colonized? As Jacques Derrida (1930–2004), the well-known French philosopher who came from a Jewish family in French Algeria, commented: 'Camus does not say who is the host and who is the guest. That is his genius.'[235]

'Jonas ou l'Artiste au Travail' ('Jonas or the Artist at work'), set in France, is clearly autobiographical. It begins as a humorous satire on literary and artistic society in Paris. Gilbert Jonas is a painter, exploited by his dealer, cultivated by his acquaintances for social prestige. He has little time to paint, and little space in an apartment filled with babies, canvases and visitors. He finds himself continually solicited to support worthy causes, to denounce injustices: *he signed only protests that claimed to be nonpartisan. But everyone claimed this worthy independence.*[236] His situation is like that of Camus in the early 1950s. While he still found time to join political protests against Franco's Spain, other demands were a burden. In a letter to a journalist, from 15 February 1951, Camus sent excuses for not being able to see him: *To do everything I would need three lives and several hearts… . I have neither the time nor the personal leisure to see my friends as I would like.*[237] Jonas has several casual love affairs and spends most of his time in bars. He returns home to build a loft in the apartment, where he can be alone and yet hear his family below him. When he falls, unconscious, from the loft, he leaves a canvas with one word painted on it. No one can tell *whether it should be read independent or interdependent* (in French *solitaire* -solitary or *solidaire* - in solidarity).[238] Jonas' loft is a humorous symbol of the artist's balance as Camus defines it in his Nobel prize acceptance speech: *The artist fashions himself in that ceaseless oscillation from himself to others, midway between the beauty he cannot do without and the community from which he cannot tear himself.*[239]

In 'La Pierre qui Pousse' ('The Growing Stone') a French engineer, D'Arrast, has come to Brazil to construct a dam. He has rejected his bourgeois culture, but cannot feel at home among the natives. After he attends a *macamba* festival, he goes to a religious procession where one of the Brazilians, attempting to carry a heavy rock to the church, stumbles and falls. D'Arrast picks up the rock, and carries it, not to the church but to a native cabin. While no one understands his action, for him it is a way to overcome temporarily his feeling of exile and solitude. Like Camus in Algeria, D'Arrast in Brazil cannot be part of either the native community or the bourgeois elite. Like Clamence in *The Fall*, D'Arrast had felt that *someone was about to die because of me*.[240] Unlike Clamence, however, in carrying the stone, D'Arrast finds a penance within a community, but he will need to return to France.

Perhaps as a way to find relief from what was happening in Algeria, Camus remained active with the theatre. In June 1957 he directed plays for the Festival in Angers: his *Caligula* (in a revised version) and *The Knight from Olmedo* by Lope de Vega (1562–1635), the Spanish Renaissance dramatist, in his translation (with help from Maria Casarès). Afterwards he commented in his notebook: *Angers festival ended. Happy fatigue. Life, marvellous life, its injustice, its glory, its passion, its fights, life begins again. Still have force to love everything and create everything*.[241] He was clearly happier working with people in the theatre than with intellectuals. He particularly liked being part of a team and working physically. As a director he was always active in rehearsals, jumping on stage frequently to suggest movements to the actors. He wanted to have his own theatre, where he could present foreign plays, classical French plays and modern French ones.

In 1957 Manès Sperber (1905–1984), a novelist and editor, conceived the idea of publishing in one volume Arthur Koestler's essay 'Reflections on Hanging' and a new essay by Camus, 'Reflections on the Guillotine'. Catherine Sellers helped Camus with his research. The volume was published in 1957 under the title *Réflexions sur la peine capitale* (*Reflections on Capital Punishment*). Camus' essay begins with a story he learned from his mother and used in *The Stranger*, of his father who attended the execution of a particularly vicious criminal, but returned home to vomit: *He had just discovered the reality hidden under the noble phrases with which it was masked... . he could think of nothing but that quivering body that had just been dropped on to a board to have its head cut off.* Camus' position is not, he says, based on any *flabby pity*, as he is willing to accept sentences of hard labour. (Then if the criminal wants to die, he can kill himself.) Camus rejects the argument that capital punishment has an exemplary value; if society really believed that, they would exhibit the heads of the guillotined criminals, or put the execution on television. Among his other arguments are: the innocent may be mistakenly executed; juries are unreliable. Essentially Camus' position is philosophical, an echo of many of his earlier essays: *No one of us can lay claim to absolute innocence. Capital punishment upsets the only indisputable human solidarity – our solidarity against death.*[242]

During October 1957 Camus learned that he would receive the Nobel Prize in Literature; at 44 he was the youngest recipient, except for Kipling who had been honoured when he was 43. Camus's first reaction was to say that it should have been given to Malraux. He still had doubts about his own writing. In August 1957 he had written: *For the first time, after reading* Crime and Punishment *absolute doubt about my vocation. I am seriously thinking of giving up.*[243] The next year, in a preface to the republication of *The Wrong Side and the Right Side* he said that a man's work is an attempt to rediscover *those two or three great and simple images in whose presence his heart first opened.* After 20 years of writing, he felt that his *work has not even begun.*[244] Undoubtedly the negative criticism of his work, especially after *The Rebel*, reinforced his natural doubts about his ability.

Critics from both the Right and the Left thought that the Swedish academy had crowned a 'finished work', that Camus no longer had anything to say. As he was not a partisan of

French Algeria, awarding him the Nobel Prize was considered by many on the Right as 'a strange and new form of interference' in the internal affairs of France. Worse, Pascal Pia, who had supported Camus in 1939, wrote that far from being a rebel, Camus was now a 'lay saint'. Camus wrote on the 19th of October: *frightened by what has happened and that I didn't ask for. And to add to that attacks so low that they break my heart.*[245]

At first he did not want to attend the Nobel ceremonies, but Gallimard convinced him to go. When he went to Stockholm in December, he was in poor physical health and his doctor forbade him to fly. He also felt psychologically harassed by the criticisms of his position on Algeria from both the Right and the Left. Politically, at the end of 1957, there was also the tension of the Cold War and his refusal, unlike most of the left-wing intellectuals in France, to support the Soviet Union. To add to his physical and mental tensions, he faced new problems in his personal life. He could not talk about the Nobel ceremonies with Maria Casarès or Catherine Sellers, neither of whom could be invited to Stockholm. There was also a new love interest, a young woman of 22 whom Camus met in 1957, and whom he calls simply 'Mi' in his notebooks. She was Danish, studying art in Paris. Camus took Francine to Stockholm, telling Mi and Catherine Sellers that Francine had suffered through the bad times and deserved one good time. To a cousin he wrote that he had never stopped loving Francine in his own bad way.[246]

Camus gave a lecture at the University of Upsala as well as a Nobel Prize acceptance speech in Stockholm. The theme running through both talks concerned the balance an artist must try to attain between the need to withdraw to write and the need to be part of society. In Upsala he criticizes both art-for-art's sake and the socialist realism of the Soviet Union: *art is neither complete rejection nor complete acceptance of what is. The artist can neither turn away from the time in which he lives nor lose himself in it.*[247]

When he was interviewed in Stockholm at the time of the ceremony for the Nobel Prize, an Algerian student interrupted and insulted him. Asked about his position on Algeria, Camus replied: *At this moment bombs are being thrown into the streetcars in Algiers. My mother might be in one of those streetcars. If that's justice, I prefer my mother.* Camus's reply was cut to 'I prefer my mother to justice'. While the phrase was used by the Left to attack him, in 2005 Abdelaziz Bouteflika, president of Algeria, told Jean Daniel: 'You know how I am sure that Camus is a real child of Algeria? It's when he said that if his mother was attacked, he would prefer to defend her rather than justice. Well, that's exactly how I feel, what I would do, and I don't know why Camus would not have had the right to say it.'[248]

By 1957 the Algerian conflict was clearly a war. The French forces were without pity, and engaged in a policy of torture. The Algerian nationalists launched a campaign of urban terrorism. Saadi Yacef, a terrorist leader, interviewed in 2007, said of the FLN strategy: 'We killed women, yes, and took fetuses out of their wombs. But ours was for liberation. This was our only means against a cruel enemy.'[249] In metropolitan France the war in Algeria was always present in the newspapers and discussions. Cars in Paris honked their horns in a rhythm to AL-GÉ-RIE FRAN-ÇAISE. The fate of Algeria aroused passions. As children the French had studied the history of French Algeria; they often felt as if the glory of France depended on retaining the colony.

In 1958 Camus finished *Actuelles III: Chroniques*

algériennes 1939–1958 ('Contemporary articles III: Algerian reports 1939–1958'). In the 'Preface to Algerian Reports', dated March-April 1958, he says that he cannot side with the French government that was trying to keep Algeria part of France while oppressing the demands of the native people, but he *cannot approve either a policy of surrender that would abandon the Arab people to an even greater poverty, tear the French in Algeria from their century-old roots, and favour, to no one's advantage, the new imperialism now threatening the liberty of France and of the West.* He was aware that his position would satisfy neither the French settlers nor the Muslim population. He wanted to avoid bloodshed and torture, utilized by both sides in the conflict: *to win wars it is better to suffer certain injustices than to commit them.* He knows that colonialism is over. What is needed among the French Algerians now is not feeling guilty but repairing injustices. What he cannot accept is negotiation with the FLN, as that would lead to independence under relentless military leaders and the eviction of 1,200,000 Europeans. He advocates an Algeria of federated settlements linked to France, much better than an *Algeria linked to an empire of Islam which would bring the Arab peoples only increased poverty and suffering.* Camus insists that the Algerian French are, *in the strongest meaning of the word, natives,* that there has never been an Algerian nation, and that *a purely Arab Algeria could not achieve the economic independence without which political independence is but a deception.* He sees the demand for independence as a part of a new Arab imperialism, which Russia uses for its anti-Western strategy. He favours a plan to have two sections, one metropolitan, one Algerian, in the French parliament. The Muslim population would retain their identity as an independent people but within a larger French political entity. If such a plan is not adopted *the consequences will be dreadful for the Arabs and for the French*. This is, he writes, his last comment, after which he will resume his silence.[250]

The volume was already at the printers when, 13 May 1958, a committee of right-wing French Algerian settlers called on their supporters to demonstrate against the FLN. The situation rapidly degenerated into a civil war. The settlers launched an appeal to General de Gaulle, then in retirement, who agreed to form a government, and went to Algiers 4 June, where he told the French Algerians 'I have understood you'. Camus had little confidence in de Gaulle. He hesitated to publish 'Algerian Reports', but decided that the positions and solutions he suggested should be made known. He still had, he said, *great hopes as well as fears*. He seems to have remained optimistic enough to think he might contribute to *defining the future* of his country.[251] 'Algerian Reports' did not sell well.

When he prepared his notebooks from August 1954 to July 1958 for publication, Camus appended to them an undated letter to a long-time friend, Jean Amrouche (1906–1962), a Berber Christian essayist and poet, a *brother born under the same sky*. Amrouche felt by 1955 that French Algeria was no longer possible. Camus disagreed with Amrouche's espousal of FLN policies: *No cause even if it was innocent and just would make me disassociate myself from my mother, who is the greatest cause that I know in this world*. He will no longer try to make *a voice of reason* heard publicly.[252] In 1958 Amrouche wrote a strong condemnation of French Algeria. Camus would no longer consider him a friend.

In a message to Charles Poncet 4 August 1958 Camus wrote: *Like you I think it is now undoubtedly too late for Algeria. I didn't say so in my book … because we must leave some chance.* By that time Poncet felt that Camus was 'short-sighted', removed from the realities in Algeria.[253] His silence, however, when there was no position he could take, may now seem the best way that he could have to express his feelings. He continued to be involved in helping individuals. He wrote letters to the government, before and after de Gaulle came to power, asking for mercy for various Muslims. Often he helped Yves Dechezelles in his work as a civil rights lawyer. He intervened in more than 150 cases of Algerians condemned for various terrorist acts.

Jean Daniel reports what Camus said to him at that time: *We cannot accept the FLN methods on the excuse that the methods of repression will be worse. We cannot accept a logic that goes so far as sacrificing our community. Mine, ours, is made of the non-Muslims of Algeria. Don't talk of French, Italians, Spanish or Jews. There are Muslims and there are the others.* Daniel adds that it is important to remember that Camus was never a partisan of 'French Algeria', never justified French colonization, never underestimated the legitimacy of Algerian nationalism.[254] If his fear of a totalitarian Islamic state may seem prophetic of events in 2007, in 1958 it was for many too close to the arguments of the French Algerian extremists.

In March 1958 Camus returned to Algeria. He had always loved the sea, and as often in the past he wrote about the movement of the waves. This time, however, the sea could not make him happy. On the return trip he wrote: *Storm. Irresistible temptation to throw myself into the sea.* He then lists *stages towards a cure*: stop thinking about politics, write comedies, expect nothing from society, break habits. He even thinks of giving up smoking, as he realizes his lungs prevent him from swimming as well as he used to. He tells himself:

My job is to write my books and fight when the freedom of my family and my people is threatened.[255] Writing became his main occupation in the last 20 months of his life.

An amused Albert Camus establishes a point in 1958.

9
1958–1960: Death and The First Man

During April 1958 Camus went to the South of France with Michel and Janine Gallimard. In June they took their boat on a tour of Greece. Maria Casarès joined them for two weeks. Camus' notebooks describe the delight he felt being at sea, and visiting a number of islands, among them Lindos, Rhodes, Kos, Mykonos. Returning to Paris he felt *power and joy* in his body. In July, however, he noted his despair both at an inability to write and at the situation in Algeria: *my land lost, I am no longer worth anything.*[256]

In September he found a property to buy, with money from the Nobel Prize. It was a small house in Lourmarin, in the South of France, not far from the Isle-sur-la-Sorge, where René Char lived and where Camus had often spent holidays. The house had separate bedrooms for himself and Francine, as well as rooms for the children, and several studies. Francine's piano was brought from Paris. Lourmarin was a village of only about 600 inhabitants, where Camus soon made friends among the local people. Mi lived nearby, and Camus saw her often. Sometimes he travelled in the south of France, with Mi or with René Char.

During 1958 he finished his adaptation for the theatre of Dostoievsky's novel, *The Possessed*, which tells of the clash of ideologies in 19th-century Russia and is critical of both the left-wing idealists and the conservative establishment's ineptitude. The theme is close to Camus' own concerns about the Soviet Union and Algeria. Camus' adaptation had 23 characters and seven scenes. He directed it in Paris and gave Catherine Sellers a major role. It ran from January to July 1959. For the 100th performance, Camus substituted real vodka for the water that one of the actors, Michel Bouquet, drank on stage, with the result that Bouquet became almost drunk and incomprehensible. When the play went on tour, Camus directed the performance in Venice and remained close to the actors. He made elaborate plans for a new theatre, with a repertory; there would be three plays performed each year in alternation, of which one would be new.

He was working regularly now on *The First Man*, which he had started as early as 1954. He went to Algiers in spring 1959 as his mother, who was very frail, was in the hospital. There was *nobility* in her features as well as resignation to her suffering. Looking at wisteria flowers he comments: *they filled my childhood with their scent … They have been more living, more present in my life than many human beings … except the one who is suffering next to me and whose silence has never ceased talking to me during half a lifetime.*[257] While in Algiers he consulted records in the National Library on his maternal family. (About his father's family he knew nothing.) His early life would be the subject of parts of *The First Man*. In November 1959 he gave himself eight months to write it and lived almost like a monk. He found the solitude crushing, but needed to force himself to work. Francine and the children came to visit Lourmarin at Christmas 1959, but he saw few other people.

Although he was unhappy being asked to comment on politics or morals and wrote: *the public aspect of my calling, which I have never liked, is becoming unbearable,*[258] he often felt obliged to comment; he answered questions for a libertarian review published in Buenos Aires, where he suggested that a united Europe, linked to Latin America, and eventually to Africa and Asia, might stand between the USSR and the United States, *when the virus of nationalism will have lost its virulence.* He continued to hope for a 'third way'.[259] Replying to questions by Jean-Claude Brisville, who was preparing a book on him, Camus claimed that he was at ease in his private relationships (surprisingly, considering his tense relationship with Francine and several other women, but he seldom spoke of his personal life), but *As to being an 'intellectual leader', it simply makes me laugh.* When asked for his reactions after the personal attacks in the press following the award of the Nobel Prize, he replied: *Oh, first of all, I felt hurt. When a man has never asked for anything in his life, and is then suddenly subjected to excessive praise and excessive blame, both praise and blame are equally painful. … Besides, these noisy events are essentially secondary.* Camus also told Brisville about his method of working. He wrote four or five hours every morning, often from notes, and liked to alternate writing with being in the open air, essential for his mental and physical health. When Brisville asked what is neglected in commentary on his work, Camus replies *Humour.*[260] In the last interview he gave, on the 20th of December 1959, for an American magazine, Camus said that French critics neglected *what is blind and instinctive in me. French criticism is initially interested in ideas.* Camus did not want to be judged as a philosopher but as an artist.[261]

While he had replied to Brisville's question about his

view of cinema with a non-committal *And you?*, Camus was tempted to act in a film and accepted an invitation to be on the jury for the Cannes film festival in 1960. He also recorded *The Fall*, reading Clamence's monologue, which was to be presented as a television programme.

In December 1959, while working on *The First Man* he made plans for his return to Paris, plans that included letters to three women, arranging to see them all - Maria Casarès, Catherine Sellers and Mi. The letter to Mi was the most passionate. According to Herbert Lottman, this young woman hoped that Camus might divorce Francine and marry her.[262] Comments in the last notebooks Camus wrote, from April to December 1959, are often concerned with love and personal morality. He notes in April that he has tried to live like others, with no success. He must accept his own nature and his *infirmities*. In June he writes that he has abandoned a moral point of view. In August he feels he has overcome indifference: *my heart lives ... thanks to Mi*. Love, he decides, will prolong youth; physical love is linked to innocence and joy. In his final notebook entry, addressed to someone he has wronged, he writes of his inability to commit himself, his need for *multiplicity*, how he has tried to detach his lovers from him. He wonders if he is capable of love. Perhaps it goes back to his first marriage: *The first person I loved and to whom I was faithful escaped from me in drugs, in betrayal. Perhaps many things are a result of that, through vanity, through fear of suffering again.*[263]

Michel and Janine Gallimard, among his closest friends for many years, visited Lourmarin. Although Camus had a train ticket to Paris, he decided to return in Michel's car. The trip started on the third of January 1960. The group (which included Janine's daughter Anne) stayed overnight near

Mâcon. According to Janine, Michel and Camus talked in the car about life insurance, their tubercular lungs, the need to make a will.[264] After lunch on the second day, approaching Sens on the way to Paris, driving on good roads with no obstacles, the car suddenly veered and struck a tree. Camus died instantly, on the fourth of January 1960 at 1:55 pm. Janine was in a state of shock, but recovered, as did Anne. Michel Gallimard died on the 10th of January. His car was a Facel Vega sports car, a model which was withdrawn in 1965 because of its many problems. The day of his death, a letter giving Camus his theatre came from Malraux's Ministry of Culture.

After his death, Camus' editors published his early novel, *A Happy Death*, collections of his journalism in *Combat* and his notebooks. The manuscript of *The First Man*, found in Camus' briefcase in the car in which he died, was not published until 1995. The title has been variously interpreted. One reading is that any French Algerian is the first man, as he has no past. French Algerians are *men of a different and undefined dawn.*[265] In a note in December 1954, Camus suggests a more universal possibility: The First Man *goes back over his whole route to discover its secret: he is not the first. Every man is the first man, no one is. That's why he throws himself at his mother's feet.*[266]

The manuscript is divided into two parts: 'Search for the Father', and 'The Son or the First Man'. There is also a series of notes and sketches to be incorporated into the manuscript. Camus writes partly to establish his relationship to his father, about whom he knows very little; he must rely on the history of the early French settlers in Algeria. Chapters alternate between the life of Jacques Cormery (the name Camus gives himself in the novel) as a child and his return to Algiers at the age of 40. He considered having chapters alternating between Jacques' voice and his mother's, *commenting on the same events but with her vocabulary of 400 words.*[267]

The First Man has more detail, more description of a precise place, more realism than in any of the fiction Camus previously wrote. It is the first work that he called a novel. Particularly striking are the descriptions of the odours of poverty. A note in the manuscript says: *the book should be heavy with things and flesh.*[268]

Along with some of the early lyrical essays, *The First Man* is the work closest to direct autobiography that Camus wrote. He normally kept his emotions at a distance. According to his daughter, Catherine, he would not have published it without masking his own feelings to a greater extent.[269] Of his mother and his uncle he writes: *he cherished them all the more for his ability to love them when he had failed to love so many who deserved it.* While he seldom mentions his brother, his uncle is a major character, perhaps a replacement for the father he did not know. The mother is the most important person in his life: he feels he is *nothing in any case next to his mother.* In a note to be added to the manuscript he writes: *His mother is Christ.*[270]

Other notes discuss Jacques' sexual life: *J. has four women at the same time and thus is leading an* empty *life; That feeling of happiness he could never experience except in what was temporary, illicit; Loves: he would have wanted them all virgin, with no past and no men… . he wanted women to be what he himself was not.* Jacques has many doubts about himself and feels he should seek forgiveness for what he has done. He sees himself as *abominable*, while his mother is *the best this world has.*[271]

Another theme is the relationship between French

Algerians and Arabs, both groups in many ways sharing the same culture, the same love of the land, a similar temperament. A fight between a Frenchman and an Arab would draw a crowd of silent Arabs which would have deprived the Frenchman *of what courage he possessed had he not been raised in this country and therefore knew that only with courage could you live here*. Jacques' mother, not considering herself French, says *The French are good people*. In a note marked *The end*, Jacques makes a plea: *Return the land. Give all the land to the poor … the immense herd of the wretched, mostly Arab and a few French, and who live and survive here through stubbornness and endurance … I will die happy.*[272] In February 1955, when he was visiting Algeria, Camus had made notes for two episodes based on the violent actions of the FLN: *He fights for the Arab cause. He is caught in an anti-French riot with his wife. He kills her to keep her from being raped, but he survives. He is judged and condemned.* Another possibility: *I fought for 20 years for them and the day they were liberated they killed my mother.*[273]

After his death, Camus' work continued to be of interest to a wide public. His books have always sold well. *The Stranger* is the best-selling book Gallimard ever published. In a poll conducted for Olivier Todd in 1995, in response to the question 'Who is the 20th-century French author, living or dead, who interests you the most?', Camus was at the top.[274] His plays, particularly *Caligula* and *The Misunderstanding*, and adaptations of *The Stranger*, are often performed in many countries. His work is as influential in Asia and Africa as it is in the West. There is a large body of interpretation of Camus's work in many languages, including Elizabeth Hawes unexpected American best seller, *Camus a Romance* (2009), in which she writes of her love for Camus as a hero for her generation. Gallimard, which published his writing in the 1960s, brought out a four-volume Pléiade edition in 2006 and 2008, to include the posthumous works.

There was a long period after 1960 in which Camus was disparaged by the critics. Militants during the 1968 uprising in Paris had little use for Camus, who seemed too moderate and traditional. As Catherine Camus explains 'French intellectuals were preoccupied with two topics: the Soviet Union and the war in Algeria.'[275] On both these issues, by denouncing totalitarianism and advocating a multicultural Algeria, Camus antagonized many. For this reason publication of *The First Man* was delayed for years. After the fall of the Berlin Wall in 1989, many French intellectuals began to reexamine their commitment to Revolution and Communism; Camus' reputation began to recover.

Many Muslim writers in Algeria appreciate Camus' writing for its honesty. It is seen as linked sensually to the country; his early criticism of colonial policy is respected, as is his analysis of man and society, although his wish to keep a federation of France and Algeria was unrealistic. The national daily newspaper, *El Moudjahid*, in 1990, introducing an article on the 45th anniversary of the Sétif revolt, 8 May, cited a 'beautiful paragraph by Camus: *Algeria is plunged into an economic and political crisis. In this admirable country which an incomparable spring is right now covering with its flowers and its light, a people is suffering*'.[276]

Camus is now often regarded as an Algerian writer, someone who better understood the complexities of Algeria than those who only perceived a struggle for liberation. His position on Algeria can be read differently with the rise of terrorism. Benjamin Stora (1950–), a historian and author of several major works on Algeria, said, 'Camus refuses to think in systems and introduces into political action a human feeling. As Camus wrote in January 1956, *No matter how old and deep are the origins of the Algerian tragedy, one fact remains: no cause ever justifies the death of an innocent being... . I am*, more than ever, close to him.'[277] Daniel Leconte, writing of misinterpreted history since Algerian independence, suggests that both French and Algerians should be 'Camusians', trying to build a common memory that will permit them to live together.[278] David Carroll's *Camus the Algerian* is a well-argued defence of Camus' position against such left-wing critics as Edward Said, Conor Cruise O'Brien and Frantz Fanon.[279]

Max Gallo (1932–), a French historian, finds in Camus' ethics as a journalist for *Combat* a message for today on the 'role of communication and the responsibilities of journalists'.[280] A younger philosopher, Michel Onfray (1959 -) holding left-wing libertarian principles, writes: 'Between a Sartre who pays no attention to economics and an Aron who only knows economics, I choose Camus' continuing concern for reality.'[281] Camus' comments on the problems of nationalism and European unity appear particularly relevant in the 21st century.

Celebrations in January 2010, the fiftieth anniversary of Camus' death, established his continued importance in France, for both his creative literature and his critical perspective on twentieth-century political and moral concerns. Many who had at one time considered Sartre the leading voice on the political left now realized that Camus was correct in his criticism of Communism and his fears about the direction of nationalist movements in Algeria. There were numerous public conferences, special issues of magazines, and new critical and biographical studies. The president of France,

Nicolas Sarkozy, proposed moving Camus' remains from Lourmarin to the Pantheon.

Camus' plays and fiction are classic works in which the autobiographical is distanced by form, the characters and stories are infused by ethical problems that remain and are likely to remain part of our lives. Camus the Algerian who lost his country seems increasingly sympathetic and a forerunner of many displaced by decolonization and independence movements. His early writings express the post-Nietzsche world in which there is no god, but for him this did not justify claiming that all was permitted. Much of his later writing was concerned with the dangerous moral effects of such a view and how it was necessary to assert a common humanity and find alternatives to post-Nietzsche existentialism. He understood that evil, no matter how justified by arguments, remains evil, while human relations, although never pure, are the true basis of the moral life. For both his literary work and his moral position he will continue to be relevant to the contemporary world.

Notes

Abbreviations

AJ *American Journals*, tr. with notes and introduction by Hugh Lewick (New York, Paragon House Publishers: 1987).

AK King, Adele (ed), *Camus's L'Etranger: Fifty Years On* (London, Macmillan: 1992).

CAI *Carnets, 1935–1942*, tr. with introduction and notes by Philip Thody (London, Hamish Hamilton: 1963).

CAII *Carnets, 1942–1951*, tr. with introduction and notes by Philip Thody (London, Hamish Hamilton: 1966).

CAIII *Carnets III*: March 1951 - December 1959 (Paris, Gallimard, 1989).

COM *Camus at Combat*, ed. Jacqueline Lévi-Valensi, tr. Arthur Goldhammer (Princeton, Princeton University Press: 2006).

EK *Exile and the Kingdom* tr. Carol Cosman, with a foreword by Orhan Pamuk (New York, Vintage International: 2006).

FALL *The Fall*, tr. Justin O'Brien (Hamish Hamilton, London, 1957).

FM *The First Man*, tr. David Hapgood (New York, Knopf: 1995).

HL Lottman, Herbert R., *Albert Camus: a biography* (Corte Madrea, California, Gingko Press: 1997).

JD Daniel, Jean, *Avec Camus* (Paris, Gallimard: 2006).

LYR *Lyrical and Critical Essays*, tr. Ellen Conroy Kennedy, introduction and notes by Philip Thody (New York, Vintage Books, Random House: 1970).

MS *The Myth of Sisyphus and other essays*, tr. Justin O'Brien (New York, Vintage Books: 1991).

OT Todd, Olivier, *Albert Camus: une vie* (Paris, Gallimard, revised edition: 1996).

PL *Caligula and 3 Other Plays*, tr. Stuart Gilbert (New York, Vintage Books, Random House: 1962).

QI: Albert Camus, *Théâtre, Récits, Nouvelles*, ed. Roger Quilliot (Paris, Gallimard, 1961).

QII. Albert Camus, *Essais*, ed. Roger Quilliot(Paris, Gallimard, 1965).

RB *The Rebel*, tr. Anthony Bower (New York, Vintage Books: 1958).

RG Grenier, Roger, *Albert Camus: soleil et ombre* (Paris, Gallimard: 1987).

RRD *Resistance, Rebellion and Death*, tr. Justin O'Brien (London, Hamish Hamilton: 1960).

ST *The Stranger*, tr. Matthew Ward (Knopf, New York: 1996).

1. LYR 166.
2. LYR 27–9.
3. LYR 32–3.
4. CAI 1.
5. JD 134–5.

6. FM 46, 89–90, 123, 58.
7. HL 9–10.
8. FM 27–8.
9. LYR 329.
10. FM 33.
11. LYR 350, 249, 358.
12. FM 251.
13. CAII 91.
14. QII 1218, 1214.
15. CAII 29.
16. HL 59.
17. OT 83.
18. HL 71.
19. FM 204.
20. OT 1067.
21. LYR 53.
22. RG 28.
23. OT 92, 120–1.
24. OT 164.
25. HL 102.
26. QI 401.
27. HL 207.
28. CAI 22.
29. LYR 41–4.
30. OT 806.
31. OT 111.
32. Bulletin of the Camus Studies Association, 26th year, No. 81, May 2007.
33. HL 162–8.
34. Emmanuel Roblès, 'Our Youthful Years' in AK, pp. 18, 22.
35. LYR 60.

36. LYR 5–6.
37. LYR 68.
38. LYR 77–8.
39. CAI 24.
40. LYR 103.
41. *A Happy Death*, tr. Richard Howard (New York, Vintage Books: 1972), pp. 139–51.
42. CAI 38–9.
43. CAI 43, 33.
44. OT 308
45. CAI 59; ST 3.
46. CAI 58, 61, 51, 112.
47. RG 95.
48. LYR 199, 203.
49. Bulletin of the Camus Studies Association, 26th year, No. 81, May 2007.
50. CAI 76, 80–1.
51. OT 291.
52. RG 361, 96–7.
53. CAI 98.
54. OT 339–40.
55. JD 42.
56. OT 324.
57. CAI 11.
58. *A Happy Death*, tr. Richard Howard (New York, Vintage Books: 1972), p. 18.
59. ST 21.
60. ST 20.
61. ST 65.
62. ST 122–3.
63. CAI 5.

64. LYR 337 (Preface to American edition of *L'Etranger*, Germaine Brée and Carlos Lynes Jr.(eds), New York, Appleton-Century Crofts: 1955).

65. CAI 18.

66. LYR 336.

67. COM 278 (17 January 1947).

68. OT 328.

69. CAI 107.

70. CAI 151, editor's note.

71. RG 117.

72. Djemaï, Abdelkader, *Camus à Oran* (Paris, Michalon: 1995), pp. 75 and 100.

73. MS 3, 21, 54.

74. MS 69, 92, 12 123.

75. OT 372.

76. MS 74.

77. LYR 118.

78. CAII 12.

79. HL 272.

80. CAII 23–5, 44.

81. CAII 38.

82. CAII 35.

83. COM 90 (27 October 1944).

84. OT 427, 272.

85. CAII 4.

86. HL 313, OT 461–2.

87. PL 134, vii-viii.

88. PL vii.

89. OT 476.

90. QII 1464.

91. OT 1095.

92. OT 485.

93. COM 118 (22 November 1944).

94. HL 350.

95. COM 192 (14 April 1945).

96. OT 482, 537.

97. AK 10.

98. HL 398.

99. FM 14.

100. JD 14.

101. COM 16 (24 August 1944); COM 83 (21 October 1944).

102. COM 13 (21 August 1944).

103. COM 191 (10 April 1945); COM 254 (15 November 1945); COM 55 (1 October 1944); COM 218 (25 May 1945); COM 141 (15 December 1944).

104. COM 100 (3 November 1944).

105. COM 172 (16 February 1945).

106. COM 90 (25 October 1944).

107. COM 163–4 (5 January 1945); COM 169 (11 January 1945); COM 233 (2 August 1945).

108. *Albert Camus: Between Hell and Reason: Essays from the Resistance Newspaper* Combat, *1944–1947*, selected and tr. Alexandre de Gramont (Hanover, NH, Wesleyan University Press: 1991), pp. 28–9.

109. COM 70 (11 October 1944); COM 200 (13–14 May 1945).

110. COM 205 (16 May 1945); COM 207 (18 May 1945); COM 215–6 (23 May 1945).

111. COM 212–3 (20–21 May 1945); COM 227 (15 June 1945).

112. COM 236 (8 August 1945); JD 31.

113. COM 23 (31 August 1944); COM 119 (22 November 1944).

114. LYR 359, interview with Jean-Claude Brisville.

115. PL 8, 72, vi.

116. CAI 77.

117. EK 93, 92.

118. HL 389–90.

119. OT 828.

120. OT 547.

121. RRD 51.

122. QII 1597.

123. CAII 67.

124. AJ 36.

125. OT 567–8.

126. LYR, 'Rains of New York' 184; AJ 41.

127. COM 260–2 (20–21 November 1946).

128. HL 459–60.

129. COM 269 (23 November 1946).

130. COM 258 (19 November 1946).

131. Judt, Tony, *The Burden of Responsibility: Blum, Camus, Aron, and the French Twentieth Century* (Chicago, University of Chicago Press: 1998), p. 115.

132. CAII 95.

133. OT 586–7.

134. CAII 27.

135. CAII 78, 93.

136. COM 305, editor's note.

137. COM 286 (30 April 1947).

138. COM 289 (7 May 1947).

139. CAII 193, editor's note.

140. CA II 89.

141. *The Plague* in *The Collected Fiction of Albert Camus*, tr. Stuart Gilbert (London, Hamish Hamilton: 1960), p. 250.

142. *The Plague*, p.102.
143. Djemai, Abdelkader, *Camus à Oran* (Paris, Michalon: 1995), pp. 86 -100.
144. LYR 338, editor's note.
145. CAII 167.
146. LYR 13, 340.
147. CAII 137.
148. LYR 353, 159.
149. COM 308 (25–6 December 1948).
150. CAII 100–1, 103–4, 129.
151. HL 457.
152. LYR 155–61.
153. LYR 145.
154. COM 309 (14 March 1949).
155. In *Correspondance (1946–1959)* (Paris, Gallimard, 2007), quoted on www.gallimard.fr/catalog.
156. Emmanuel Roblès, 'Our Youthful Years' in AK p. 21.
157. CAII 143, 149; OT 649–59.
158. HL 466.
159. PL viii.
160. OT 656.
161. COM 299–301 (25 November 1948).
162. QII 788.
163. HL 489.
164. AJ 62, 112, 93, 99, 114, 142.
165. CAII 146.
166. AII 88.
167. PL 288.
168. JD 132.
169. PL 259, 245, 297.
170. CAII 102.
171. PL x.

172. CAII 78, 107, 159.
173. CAII 162–3.
174. LYR 9.
175. OT 738.
176. RB 262–3.
177. RB 294, 306.
178. OT 766
179. CAIII 30.
180. OT 749.
181. HL 757.
182. QII 772.
183. OT 778.
184. OT 789.
185. Milan Kundera, 'Die Weltliteratur'. *The New Yorker*, 8 January 2007, p. 34.
186. FM 317.
187. 'The Artist and his time', republished in MS 207, 208, 211, 212.
188. QII 780.
189. QII 1629.
190. CAIII 59, 103.
191. LYR 118.
192. OT 810–13.
193. CAIII 136–7, 145.
194. CAIII 146–7.
195. CAI, editor's introduction, v-vi.
196. LYR 6.
197. PL vi-x.
198. QII 1491.
199. CAIII 101–2, 113, 109, 128.
200. CAIII 127.
201. JD 84.

202. CAIII 163–4.
203. OT 853, letter to Charles Poncet, December 1955.
204. OT 851, *L'Express* 8 November 1955.
205. JD 55–9.
206. CAI, editor's note, vii.
207. CAIII 125.
208. Fall 100.
209. RB 243.
210. CAIII 147.
211. OT 877.
212. CAIII 240–1.
213. *Temps Modernes* 'Pour tout vous dire' 372; Fall 21.
214. Fall 107.
215. QII 1746.
216. OT 917.
217. CAIII 197.
218. Bulletin of the Camus Studies Association, 26th year, No. 81, May 2007; HL 520.
219. CAIII 111.
220. HL 553.
221. JD 59.
222. CAIII 291–2.
223. RRD 91.
224. OT 825.
225. OT 848, 852.
226. CAIII 182.
227. CAIII 182.
228. http://www.alger-roi.net/Alger/portraits/pages_liees/0181_camus_impossible_treve_pn62.htm
229. RRD 97
230. CAIII 214.
231. QI 2039

232. OT 902.
233. EK 86.
234. CAIII 174.
235. Quoted in David Carroll, *Camus the Algerian: Colonialism, Terrorism, Justice* (New York: Columbia University Press, 2007)p. 73.
236. EK 104.
237. CAIII 76.
238. EK 104, 123.
239. RRD 196.
240. EK 146.
241. CAIII 203.
242. RRD 127, 129, 158.
243. CAIII 207.
244. LYR 17.
245. CAIII 214.
246. OT 978, 954.
247. RRD 186–7.
248. JD 140.
249. *International Herald Tribune*, 20 June 2007, p. 2.
250. RRD 81, 83, 87, 90, 104, 110.
251. QII 889.
252. CAIII 137–8.
253. OT 993, 996.
254. JD 60, 76–7.
255. CAIII 220–224.
256. CAIII 233, 251.
257. CAIII 262–3.
258. LYR 358.
259. OT 1029.
260. LYR 359, 365, 362.
261. QII 1925.

262. HL xiv.

263. CAIII 266, 268, 271, 279.

264. HL 698.

265. FM 319.

266. CAIII 142.

267. FM 313.

268. FM 105.

269. FM vii.

270. FM 129, 278, 294.

271. FM 296, 301, 315, 310.

272. FM 280, 73, 318.

273. CAIII 154.

274. OT 1042–3.

275. FM vi.

276. Christiane Achour 'Camus and Algerian Writers' in AK p.89.

277. Benjamin Stora, 'Mon journal', *Libération*, 3–4 November 2007, p. 27.

278. Daniel Leconte, *Camus si tu savais* (Paris: Seuil, 2006), p. lxi.

279. David Carroll, *Camus the Algerian: Colonialism, Terrorism, Justice* (New York: Columbia University Press, 2007).

280. Max Gallo, 'Une véritable éthique du journalisme', *Le Nouvel Observateur*, 30 November 2007, p. 48.

281. 'Les débats de l'Obs', *Le Nouvel Observateur*, 8–14 March 2007), p. 114.

Works in French

Published in Camus's lifetime, all by Gallimard, Paris, unless otherwise noted. Translations in parentheses, italicizing if published as books in English.

1937   *L'Envers et l'Endroit* (Charlot, Algiers, reedited Paris, 1958) (*The Wrong Side and the Right Side*)

1938   *Noces* (Charlot, Algiers, reedited Paris, 1949) (*Nuptials*)

1942   *L'Etranger* (*The Stranger* or *The Outsider*)
       Le Mythe de Sisyphe (*The Myth of Sisyphus*)

1944   *Caligula*
       Le Malentendu (*Cross Purposes* or *The Misunderstanding*)

1945   *Lettres à un Ami Allemand* (*Letters to a German Friend*)

1947   *La Peste* (*The Plague*)

1948   *L'Etat de Siège* (*State of Siege*)

1950   *Les Justes* (*The Just Assassins*)
       Actuelles I – Chroniques 1944–1948 ('Contemporary Articles I')

1951   *L'Homme Révolté* (*The Rebel*)

1953 *Actuelles II – Chroniques 1948–1953* ('Contemporary Articles II')
1954 *L'Eté (Summer)*
1956 *La Chute (The Fall)*
1957 *L'Exil et le Royaume (Exile and the Kingdom)*
      'Réflexions sur la guillotine', in *Réflexions sur la peine capitale* (Calman Levy, Paris. with Arthur Koestler) ('Reflections on the guillotine', in *Reflections on capital punishment*)
1958 *Actuelles III – Chroniques algériennes 1939–1958* ('Contemporary articles III: Algerian Reports')
      Discours de Suède (Nobel Prize Acceptance Speech)

Posthumous publications

1961 The prestigious Pléiade collection at Gallimard brought out a two-volume set of Camus's work in the 1960s, edited with notes by Roger Quilliot. Volume I: *Théâtre, Récits, Nouvelles* (1961). Volume II: *Essais* (1965).
1962 *Carnets I: Mai 1935–Février 1942 (Notebooks* or *Carnets)*
1964 *Carnets II: Janvier 1942–Mars 1951 (Notebooks* or *Carnets)*
1971 *La Mort Heureuse (A Happy Death)*
1978 *Journaux de voyage (American journals)*
1989 *Carnets III*: March 1951–December 1959
1995 *Le Premier Homme (The First Man)*
2002 *Camus à Combat*, ed. Jacqueline Lévi-Valensi (*Camus at Combat*)
2006 A four-volume set of Camus's work, in the Pleiade
–08   collection, edited by Jacqueline Lévi-Valensi until her death and then by Raymond Gay-Crosier, includes

the posthumous works and newly authenticated
journalism. *Tome I: 1931–1944* (2007), *Tome II:
1944–48* (2006), *Tome III: 1949–1956* (2008), *Tome IV:
1957–1960* (2008).

Translations used
Fiction and Plays

The Stranger, tr. Matthew Ward (Knopf, New York: 1996).

The Collected Fiction of Albert Camus (Hamish Hamilton,
London: 1960). Cited for *The Plague* tr. Stuart Gilbert.

The Fall, tr. Justin O'Brien (Hamish Hamilton, London:
1957).

Exile and the Kingdom, tr. Carol Cosman, with a foreword
by Orhan Pamuk (Vintage International, New York:
2006).

A Happy Death, tr. Richard Howard (Vintage Books, New
York: 1972).

The First Man, tr. David Hapgood (Vintage Books, New
York: 1996). Editor's note by Catherine Camus.

Caligula and 3 Other Plays, tr. Stuart Gilbert (Vintage
Books, New York: 1962). Includes *Caligula*, *The
Misunderstanding*, *State of Siege*, *The Just Assassins*,
and a preface by Camus, tr. Justin O'Brien.

Essays

Lyrical and Critical Essays, tr. Ellen Conroy Kennedy,
introduction and notes, Philip Thody (Vintage Books,
New York: 1970). Includes *The Wrong Side and the
Right Side*, *Nuptials*, *Summer*, plus Critical Essays
(on Sartre, Parain, Gide, Martin du Gard, Melville,
Faulkner, Char, Grenier), preface to *The Stranger* (1956),
letters, three interviews.

The Myth of Sisyphus and other essays, tr. Justin O'Brien
    (Vintage Books, New York: 1991; first edition by Alfred
    Knopf in 1955). Includes some essays from *Summer*:
    'The Minotaur, or the stop in Oran', 'Helen's Exile',
    'Return to Tipasa'. Also 'Summer in Algiers' (From
    Nuptials) and 'The Artist and his Time'(from *Actuelles
    II*).
The Rebel, tr. Anthony Bower, foreword by Sir Herbert
    Read (Vintage Books, New York: 1958).
Resistance, Rebellion and Death, tr. Justin O'Brien (Hamish
    Hamilton, London: 1960). Includes *Letters to a German
    Friend*, articles from *Combat*, miscellaneous articles,
    mostly from *Actuelles I, II, III*, including a number
    from 'Algerian Reports', *Reflections on the Guillotine*,
    Nobel Prize Acceptance Speech, plus a lecture given
    at the University of Upsala in December 1957. (These
    are the essays Camus chose to be included in an
    English-language edition of his shorter works.)
Carnets, 1935–1942, tr. with introduction and notes, Philip
    Thody (Hamish Hamilton, London: 1963). (New York
    edition is entitled *Notebooks, 1935–1942*.)
Carnets, 1942–1951, tr. with introduction and notes by
    Philip Thody (Hamish Hamilton, London: 1966. (New
    York edition is entitled *Notebooks, 1942–1951*.)
American Journals, tr. with notes by Hugh Lewick
    (Paragon House Publishers, New York: 1987. Includes
    introduction to the French edition by Roger Quilliot,
    The United States (March-May 1946) and *South
    America* (June-August 1949).
*Albert Camus: Between Hell and Reason: Essays from
    the Resistance Newspaper* Combat, *1944–1947*, tr.

Alexandre de Gramont (Wesleyan University Press, Hanover: 1991).

Camus at Combat, ed. Jacqueline Lévi-Valensi, tr. Arthur Goldhammer (Princeton University Press, Princeton: 2006).

Other translations

Penguin Modern Classics has published a uniform set of translations (some new, some republished):

The Myth of Sisyphus, tr. Justin O'Brien, 2000

The Fall, tr. Robin Buss, 2006

The Outsider, tr. Joseph Laredo, 2000

The First Man, tr. David Hapgood, 2001

The Plague, tr. Robin Buss, 2002

The Exile and the Kingdom, tr. Carol Cosman, 2006

A Happy Death, tr. Richard Howard, 2002

The Rebel, tr. Anthony Bower, 2000

Caligula and Other Plays, 2006, tr. Stuart Gilbert

Notebooks 1951–1959, tr. Ryan Bloom, Chicago, Ivan R. Dee, 2008

Further Reading

Biographies

Djemaï, Abdelkader, *Camus à Oran* (Michalon, Paris: 1995). An illustrated story of Camus's life in Oran, particularly January 1941 to July 1942.

Grenier, Roger, *Albert Camus: soleil et ombre* (Gallimard, Paris: 1987). Grenier writes of Camus's work, not his life. He includes discussion of Camus's critical essays and his translations.

Hawes, Elizabeth, *Camus, a Romance* (Grove Press, New York: 2009). A personal account of the author's search to understand Camus as a man and as a writer.

Lenzini, José, *Les derniers jours de la vie d'Albert Camus* (Actes Sud, Paris: 2009). A story of the last days of Camus's life.

Lottman, Herbert R., *Albert Camus: a biography* (Gingko Press, Corte Madrea, California: 1997 (first published New York, Doubleday: 1979). This is a thorough investigation of Camus's life, often the source for later writers on Camus. As it was written before the death of Francine Camus, it does not discuss Camus's personal life in detail.

McCarthy, Patrick, *Camus: A Critical Study of His Life and Work*, (Hamish Hamilton, London: 1982). This biography includes some new interviews and a discussion of Camus's politics in relation to his fiction.

Todd, Olivier, *Albert Camus: une vie* (Gallimard, Paris: revised edition: 1996). English translation, *Albert Camus: A Life*, Knopf, New York: 1997). Citations here are from the French edition, as the English translation is abridged. Todd is the most complete biography to date. It discusses Camus's personal life in more detail than the earlier biographers could do, and includes interviews with many who knew Camus and excerpts from letters, both personal and political, throughout Camus's life.

Bibliographies

Albert Camus, Bibliography Project, microfilm established by Robert F. Roeming, University of Wisconsin, 1968–2000.

Web site, since 2000, coordinated by Professor Raymond Gay-Crosier: www.clas.ufl.edu/users/gaycros/Bibliog.htm

Critical studies in English

Aronson, Ronald, *Camus and Sartre: The Story of a Friendship and the Quarrel that Ended it* (University of Chicago Press, Chicago and London: 2004).

Bloom, Harold (ed.), *Albert Camus: Modern Critical Views* (New York, Chelsea House Publishers: 1989). Some well-known American academic scholars look at Camus, and take a critical view of his work. A useful essay is English Showalter, Jr., 'The Growing Stone: Reconciliation and Conclusion' (pp. 139–155).

Carroll, David, *Albert Camus the Algerian* (Columbia University Press, New York: 2007). A defence of Camus in reponse to critics who attribute to him a racially biased perpective on Algeria.

Fitch, Brian, *"The Fall", a Matter of Guilt* (Twayne, New York: 1995).

Freeman, E. *The Theatre of Albert Camus* (Methuen, London: 1971).

Golomb, Jacob, *In Search of Authenticity: From Kierkegaard to Camus* (Routledge, London: 1995).

Hughes, Edward (ed.), *The Cambridge Companion to Camus* (Cambridge University Press, Cambridge: 2007).

Isaac, Jeffrey, *Arendt, Camus and Modern Rebellion* (Yale University Press, New Haven: 1992). Comparisons of the philosophical and ethical thought of Camus and Hannah Arendt.

Judt, Tony, *The Burden of Responsibility: Blum, Camus, Aron, and the French Twentieth Century* (University of Chicago Press, Chicago: 1998). An excellent analysis of Camus's thought, a useful corrective to the attacks of Sartre's followers.

King, Adele (ed.), *L'Etranger: Fifty Years On* (Macmillan, London: 1992). Includes textual studies, comparative studies, and essays on how *The Stranger* has influenced writers from Samoa, India, Algeria and France.

Rizzuto, Anthony, *Camus: Love and Sexuality* (University Press of Florida, Gainesville: 1998).

Critical studies in French

Champigny, Robert, *Sur un héros païen* (Gallimard, Paris: 1959). An early study of Meursault in *The Stranger* as an epicurean hero.

Chaulet-Achour, Christiane, *Albert Camus, Alger* (Biarritz, Séguier: 1998). Camus in relation to Algerian writing.

Daniel, Jean, *Avec Camus* (Gallimard, Paris: 2006). An excellent memoir and study of Camus's ethics of journalism.

Gay-Crosier, Raymond (ed.), *Textes, intertextes, contextes. Autour de La Chute* (Lettres Modernes, Paris: 1993).

Grenier, Jean, *Albert Camus: souvenirs* (Gallimard, Paris: 1968). Memoirs by Camus's mentor in Algiers and life-long friend.

Guérin, Jeanvyes, editor, *Dictionnaire Camus* (Robert Laffont, Paris: 2009).

Leconte, Daniel, *Camus si tu savais* (Seuil, Paris: 2006). Leconte reads the recent history of Algeria and of Algerian descendants in France with reference to Camus's thought.

Lévi-Valensi, Jacqueline (ed.), *Albert Camus et le théâtre* (Imec, Paris: 1992).

Lévi-Valensi, Jacqueline, *Albert Camus ou la naissance d'un romancier* (Gallimard, Paris: 2006). A detailed account of Camus's varied writings before *The Stranger*.

Background reading

Appignanesi, Lisa, *Simone de Beauvoir* (Haus Books, London: 2005).

Beauvoir, Simone de, *Les Mandarins* (Gallimard, Paris: 1954). *The Mandarins*, tr. Leonard M. Friedman (Norton, New York: 1991).

Beauvoir, Simone de, *La force de l'age* (Gallimard, Paris: 1960). *The Prime of Life*, tr. Peter Green (Penguin, London: 1965). Her early life with Sartre and during the Second World War.

Beauvoir, Simone de, *La force des choses* (Gallimard, Paris: 1963). *Force of Circumstance*, tr. Richard Howard (Penguin, London: 1968). Description of post-war politics, the relationship of Beauvoir and Sartre to Camus, and the Algerian struggle.

Drake, David, *Sartre* (Haus Books, London: 2005).

Horne, Alastair, *A Savage War of Peace* (Viking, New York: 1978).

Judt, Tony, *Postwar: A History of Europe since 1945* (Penguin, London: 2005).

Le Sueur, James D., *Uncivil War: Intellectuals and Identity Politics during the decolonization of Algeria* (University of Nebraska Press, Lincoln: 2005).

Lottman, Herbert R. *The Left Bank: Writers, Artists and Politics from the Popular Front to the Cold War* (University of Chicago Press, Chicago: 1982).

Memmi, Albert, *The Colonizer and the Colonized*, tr. Howard Greenfeld, introduction by Jean-Paul Sartre (Beacon Press, Boston: 1965).

Shepard, Todd, *The Invention of Decolonization: The Algerian War and the Remaking of France* (Cornell University Press, Ithaca: 2006).

Stora, Benjamin, *Algeria 1830–2000* (Cornell University Press, Ithaca: 2001).

Tillion, Germaine, *L'Algérie en 1957* (Editions de Minuit, Paris: 1957).

Windrow, Martin, *The Algerian War 1954–62* (Osprey, London: 1997).

Index